Learning to use statistical tests in psychology: a student's guide

Judith Greene
and
Manuela d'Oliveira

OPEN UNIVERSITY PRESS
Milton Keynes · Philadelphia

Open University Press
Celtic Court
22 Ballmoor
Buckingham MK18 1XW
and
1900 Frost Road, Suite 101
Bristol, PA 19007, USA

First published 1982
Reprinted 1983, 1985, 1987, 1988, 1989, 1990, 1992, 1993

British Library Cataloguing in Publication Data

Greene, Judith
  Learning to use statistical tests in psychology: a student's guide
  I. Mathematical statistics   2. Psychology
    Statistical methods
  I. Title   II. D'Oliveira, Manuela
  519.5′4′02415   QA276
  ISBN 0-335-10177-1

Printed in Great Britain by
St Edmundsbury Press Limited, Bury St Edmunds, Suffolk

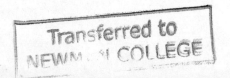

To Norman, Kate and Matthew

and

To Eduardo

Contents

Acknowledgements

Grateful acknowledgement is made to the following sources for permission to reprint the tables in this book.

Table A from F. Wilcoxon and R. A. Wilcox, *Some Rapid Approximate Statistical Procedures*, American Cyanamid Co., 1949;

Table B from R. P. Runyon and A. Haber, *Fundamentals of Behavioral Statistics*, 3rd Edn., Reading, Mass., Addison-Wesley, 1976;

Table C from M. Friedman, 'The use of ranks to avoid the assumption of normality implicit in the analysis of variance' in *Journal of the American Statistical Association*, Vol. 32, 1937;

Table D from D. V. Lindley and J. C. P. Miller, *Cambridge Elementary Statistical Tables*, 10th Edn., Cambridge University Press, 1973;

Table E from E. E. Page's article in *Journal of the American Statistical Association*, Vol. 58, 1963;

Table F from W. H. Kruskal and W. A. Wallis, 'Use of ranks in one-criterion variance analysis' in *Journal of the American Statistical Association*, Vol. 47, 1952;

Table G from A. R. Jonckheere, 'A distribution-free k-sample test against ordered alternatives' in *Biometrika*, Vol. 41 Biometrika Trustees 1954;

Table H from D. V. Lindley and J. C. P. Miller, *Cambridge Elementary Statistical Tables*, 10th Edn., Cambridge University Press, 1973;

Table I from D. V. Lindley and J. C. P. Miller, *Cambridge Elementary Statistical Tables*, 10th Edn., Cambridge University Press, 1973;

Table J from E. G. Olds, 'The 5% significance levels for sums of squares of rank differences and a correction' in *Annals of Mathematical Statistics*, Vol. 20, The Institute of Mathematical Statistics 1949;

Table K from Table VII (p.63) of R. A. Fisher and F. Yates, *Statistical Tables for Biological, Agricultural and Medical Research*, published by Longman Group Ltd, London (previously published by Oliver and Boyd Ltd, Edinburgh).

I am grateful to the Literary Executor of the late Sir Ronald A. Fisher, F.R.S. to Dr Frank Yates, F.R.S. and to Longman Group Ltd, London for permission to reprint Table VII from their book *Statistical Tables for Biological, Agricultural and Medical Research* (6th Edition, 1974).

Preface

There have been an enormous number of textbooks which have claimed to present statistics in a simple way. Despite this, many psychology students still find the whole statistical business something of a mystery.

How does this book differ from these other attempts?

We believe that virtually all books on statistics aim to given an *overall* picture of statistics. They feel obliged to start with the mathematical principles underlying probability distributions, samples and populations, and statistical testing. But, however simply these are presented, in our view they obscure the basic reasons why psychologists use statistical tests.

So we had better come clean straightway. This book sets out to achieve one single aim. This is to enable students to select appropriate statistical tests to evaluate the significance of data obtained from psychological experiments. In other words, this book is concerned with *inferential statistics* as used in psychological experimental studies.

This does not imply a cookbook approach; simply that in our experience the major problem for students is deciding which tests they should use for which experimental designs and why. Usually, once they have been given —as if by magic—the correct formula, they have little trouble in doing the actual calculations. It is for this reason that we start by describing the major characteristics of experimental design which determine the selection of statistical tests. The aim is to replace 'magic' by giving psychology students a systematic understanding of the *rationale* for choosing statistical tests.

We have concentrated on this to the exclusion of much else. Topics like descriptive statistics and the basic principles of probability are well covered in other statistical texts. Moreover, we will be concentrating on psychological *experiments* rather than other types of psychological investigation. There is nothing here about the use of surveys, observational techniques or psychometric tests of intelligence and personality. All we have included is the battery of statistical tests which are usually introduced to psychology students as part of their undergraduate laboratory course. We hope that, by aiming at a single target, we will maximize our chances of scoring a bulls-eye.

While this is definitely a 'beginners' book, it takes students from the simplest non-parametric tests, like the Wilcoxon test, through to complex Analysis of Variance designs. The principle is the same throughout: always to give the rationale for using appropriate statistical analyses for particular experimental designs. It is certainly our expectation that anyone who has mastered the why and how of the statistical tests given in this book will be in a position to understand the basic principles of statistical tests as presented in advanced textbooks of psychological statistics.

From the point of view of a teacher, the arrangement of this book may cause some problems. It is still the case that in some psychology departments the basic principles of statistics are taught separately from the practice of experimental design. It would probably be unusual, too, for all the statistical tests covered in our book to be covered in a single course. Some of the more complex Analysis of Variance designs might be reserved for advanced courses in later years.

The point is that we really mean what we say, when we call this book *Learning to Use Statistics in Psychology: A Student's Guide*. It has been designed for *students* to use on their own and to act as a *guide* for them to refer to *throughout* their experimental psychology courses.

Teachers will obviously wish to plan their own experimental design and statistics courses. We ourselves feel that it is very important for all students to start by reading the relatively short chapters 1, 2 and 3 on Introduction to Psychological Research, Experimental Design and Statistical Analysis. Given this basic reading it would be perfectly possible for a teacher to begin with the simpler non-parametric tests, as we have suggested; or alternatively to decide to go straight to the Chi-Square test; or to start with the parametric *t* tests or correlational designs, depending on the planned structure of experimental courses.

Our belief is that students with the aid of this book will feel comfortable about the basis for selecting and applying all kinds of statistical tests. We hope that teachers will wish to use a book which frees students from much of the panic usually associated with statistics. That way they should be in a far more receptive state to learn.

Study Guide for Students

The aim of this book is to explain the rationale for using statistical tests to evaluate the results of psychological experiments. You will be asked to carry out and design a number of experiments during your study of psychology. The problem is that in psychology you have to carry out these experiments on *human beings*, often other students. Unlike most physical objects, human beings are unique, each interpreting and performing whatever task you set them in a slightly different way.

You will find that the data and observations obtained from the people doing a psychological experiment are often extremely varied and that many of the things which influence their behaviour may have nothing to do with the experiment. It is for this reason that you have to sort out whether experimental results are really significant. And, as you will see, this is just what statistical tests enable you to do.

The first chapter of the book introduces you to the basic principles of psychological research; while Chapter 2 presents some important features which have to be taken into account when designing different types of psychological experiments.

You will probably be relieved to hear that Chapter 3, which introduces the basic rationale for statistics, is one of the shortest chapters. Chapter 4 is even shorter but it is *crucial* since it summarizes all you need to know in order to select an appropriate statistical test for each type of experiment. This is an aspect of using statistical tests that students often find rather puzzling, but we hope that this chapter will clear up all your worries.

All the other chapters in the book present particular statistical tests, explaining the rationale for each one, taking you 'step-by-step' through any necessary calculations and giving precise instructions about how to use the statistical tables in the Appendix.

One essential feature of this book is the *questions* which occur throughout the text. It is not enough to read the summaries presented in the *Progress Boxes*. The only way you can make sure that you understand the content of each section is to attempt the questions *before* looking up the answers at the back! It is equally important to work your way through the step-by-step instructions given for each statistical test. Otherwise, you will never gain the confidence which comes from fully understanding the rationale for a statistical test as you successfully complete the necessary arithmetic calculations.

Question 0

Which two of the chapters mentioned in this study guide are the most crucial for *selecting* the correct statistical test for analysing the results of a psychological experiment?
(Answer over page)

Let us end by making some important, and, we hope, encouraging points. The first thing to grasp is that statistical tests are not magic formulae to be turned to desperately wondering which on earth to choose. They simply follow as a natural result of the kind of experiment you have chosen to do. What makes most people give up all hope of mastering statistics is the thought that they will find themselves presented with a whole lot of numerical data without the foggiest idea of how to deal with them. But this is quite the wrong way to go about things. The important thing is to decide what experiment you want to carry out. You will find that such a decision immediately narrows your possible choice of statistical tests to only one or two, and that there are good reasons for selecting one or the other.

With statistical tests selection is all; the actual calculations are quite easy once you have understood the reasons for doing them. The aim has been to introduce the principles of using statistical tests *without referring to any mathematical concepts*. And, in order to do the calculations for the tests themselves, you will only need to know how to add, subtract, multiply, divide and square numbers. With modern pocket calculators this really should be child's play.

Good luck—and if, in spite of everything, you do find yourself getting disheartened by statistics, turn back and reread this study guide.

Answer to Question 0

Chapter 2 sets out the various types of experiments which psychologists carry out. Chapter 4 tells you which statistical text is appropriate for each type of experimental design.

Did you try to think about Question 0 before you turned to this answer. If you did *and* got the right answer, this should make you feel confident that you are following the text. If you got it wrong, then reading the answer should have given you instant illumination. At least, that is the theory. And, of course, if you didn't bother to look up the answer at all, that shows either sublime self-confidence or congenital laziness, neither of which may be ideal qualities for the reader of this book! The rest of the answers to questions are gathered together at the end of the book starting on p. 149.

CHAPTER 1

Introduction to Psychological Research

The way we propose to tackle the daunting task of introducing statistics 'without tears' is to concentrate on what statistical tests are *for*. Once you have grasped this we hope the rest will fall into place.

The first thing to consider is *why* psychologists carry out experiments. The simple answer is that they want to develop and test *theories* about human nature and experience.

Let us start by supposing that you as a psychologist have a theory about how children acquire reading skills. On the basis of this you have developed a new reading scheme which consists of a set of picture/sentence cards. Now you want to carry out some research to demonstrate whether your theory works or not. Filled with enthusiasm you find a friendly school which allows you to give your reading scheme to a group of children and to measure their reading scores at the end of term. What might be the reaction of a sceptical teacher?

Sceptical teacher How do I know the children's scores were any better after the reading scheme than they were before?

You as a researcher Well, I measured their reading scores *before* as well as *after* the reading scheme. Their scores after the scheme were higher, showing an improvement in reading.

Sceptic Can you be sure that their scores wouldn't have gone up anyway without the scheme? After all, the children were 3 months older by the time you tested them the second time.

Researcher I compared the reading scores of the children who were given the reading scheme with another group of children who didn't have the scheme. The children who were given the scheme improved more.

Sceptic How do you know that the children you gave the reading scheme to weren't better at reading anyway? Or perhaps they were worse at reading in the first place and so had more room for improvement. Or perhaps the first lot were all girls who tend to learn to read more quickly.

Researcher I tried to match my two groups of children as carefully as possible for all relevant factors, e.g. sex, intelligence, initial reading skills. As it wouldn't have been possible to match the children on all possible characteristics, I otherwise allocated them randomly to the two groups. So any differences between the groups ought to be due to my reading scheme rather than to any other factor.

Sceptic   How can you be sure that the teacher who administered the reading scheme wasn't particularly enthusiastic about it and expected improved reading scores? The other group may have got the same old bored and discouraged teacher and that's why their scores didn't go up; nothing to do with your reading scheme.

Researcher   I was particularly careful that the same teacher was responsible for teaching both groups and that he/she was given something interesting to do even with the other group of children.

Sceptic   But if you only used one teacher at one school how do I know that your reading scheme would help children in other schools?

Researcher   What I really meant to say was that I carried out the research in several schools, all in different areas and with different kinds of children.

Sceptic   How did you manage to standardize conditions in all these different schools or did you let things just happen?

Researcher   I made up some instructions telling teachers how to administer the reading tests, how many weeks to operate the scheme, how large the classes should be, and so on.

Sceptic   The more I hear you talking the more I wonder about all the variability introduced by using different children, different teachers, different schools. Individuals vary so much in their performance even from day to day. How can you be certain that the improvement in reading scores that you attribute to your reading scheme is big enough to count as a real difference between the reading scheme group and the no reading scheme group? Perhaps the results of your experiment were all due to chance fluctuations in performance.

Researcher   Ah well, I went off and did a statistical test which told me that the difference in reading scores between the two groups was unlikely to have occurred simply by chance. It was a big enough and a consistent enough difference to count as a real difference between the two groups of children.

Sceptic   Now I come to think of it, I am not really interested in crude differences between children who were given the reading scheme and those who were not. What I want to know is whether it is only children who are already fairly good at spelling who benefit from the scheme, or whether it is particularly helpful for backward spellers.

Researcher   Why didn't you say so before? I could have measured the children's initial spelling scores to see whether it was children with poor or better spelling scores who were most likely to show improvement after the reading scheme.

Sceptic   But, even if you found that better spelling scores were associated with improved reading scores, mightn't this be due to some quite different factor? Mightn't it be that children who enjoy school lessons are more likely both to be good spellers and to benefit from any new teaching scheme? So it wouldn't be spelling ability as such which was responsible for these children showing more improvement.

Researcher   It certainly is a problem to discover exactly what is behind an association between spelling and reading scores. That is why it would be a good idea to have equal numbers of poor and good spellers, and children who enjoy and who hate school lessons, in my experiment. That way I might be able to find out whether factors such as spelling abilities or attitudes to school have an effect on whether children benefit more or less from the reading scheme.

We are sure we have not covered all the possible objections which can be made to the design of experimental research. But we hope we have given you an inkling of the kinds of things that have to be taken into account. Basically they all stem from the fact that human beings each have their own peculiar quirks, past history and reactions to taking part in psychological experiments. So there may be all sorts of *irrelevant factors* affecting people's behaviour which have nothing to do with the problem the researcher is interested in.

So what is the unfortunate researcher to do? Obviously it is not possible to look at all possible factors which might affect the way children learn to read at once. Sometimes it is appropriate for psychologists to carry out an exploratory investigation in which they can observe as much as they can about ongoing behaviour. This can be a useful stage in developing a theory about what might be the most important factors affecting a particular type of behaviour. However, at some point a researcher will want to test out his theory. In order to do this, the researcher will make a *prediction* about the kind of behaviour which would be expected to occur if the theory is true. A prediction of this kind is known as the *experimental hypothesis*.

1.1   THE EXPERIMENTAL HYPOTHESIS

The first thing to notice about an experimental hypothesis is that it predicts a *relationship* between two or more events, for instance, giving children a reading scheme and their scores on a reading test. Such events are known as *variables* because they *vary* in the experimental situation. Obviously children's reading scores vary over a whole range of values, from poor reading scores to good reading scores. The reading scheme is also a variable because you as the researcher were comparing a situation in which children were either given a reading scheme or no reading scheme; in other words, the children's experience varied between reading scheme or no reading scheme.

One especially important point to notice is that, in order to carry out a test of an experimental hypothesis, it must in principle be possible for the predicted effects either to occur or *not* to occur. In our example it must be possible for the results of the reading scheme either to *support* the experimental hypothesis (i.e. that children given the reading scheme will obtain higher reading scores) or *not* to support the hypothesis (i.e. that there will be no real differences in reading scores between the children whether they are given the reading scheme or not).

This is a basic rule of experimental research. If there is no possibility that an experiment might go *against* the experimental hypothesis, then there is no point in doing the experiment at all. Consequently, an experimental hypothesis is always tested against a *null hypothesis*, which states that an experimenter will *not* find the experimental results he or she expects. According to the null hypothesis, any results found in an experiment are due to chance fluctuations in people's performance rather than to the predicted effects of the variable the experimenter is interested in. In our example, the null hypothesis would be that any differences in the children's reading scores would not be due to whether they had been given a reading scheme or not; rather they would be due to all sorts of other unknown variables which may affect children's performance on reading tests.

The next question is how to set about showing whether there is indeed a predicted relationship between two variables, that is whether the variable of reading scheme versus no reading scheme has any effect on the variable of children's reading scores. In other words, how can we demonstrate that the null hypothesis is *not* true?

1.2 MANIPULATION OF VARIABLES

The most common method of showing this in psychological experiments is for the experimenter to *manipulate* one of the variables to see whether it has an effect on the other variable. In the reading scheme experiment the researcher manipulated one variable (reading scheme or no reading scheme) to see what effect this would have on another variable (children's reading scores). If children who were given the reading scheme showed more improvement in reading scores than children given no reading scheme, then the experimenter could claim that the relationship between the two variables was in the direction predicted by the experimental hypothesis, namely that the reading scheme would improve children's reading skills.

In fact, this is a *basic experimental design:* to allocate people to *experimental conditions* representing different conditions for one of the variables (e.g. reading scheme versus no reading scheme). In this way a comparison can be made between the experimental conditions to see what effect manipulating the reading scheme variable has on the other variable of reading scores.

We should now like to introduce the terminology of *independent variables* and *dependent variables*. The variable which the researcher manipulates is known as the *independent variable*. This is because the experimental conditions to test this variable are set up *independently* before the experiment even begins. The second variable, the reading test scores, is known as the *dependent variable*. The is because the reading scores are *dependent* on the way in which the experimenter manipulates the independent variable of the reading scheme.

Question 1

Suppose a psychologist designs an experiment to test an experimental hypothesis that people will take less time to read a text with illustrations than the same text without illustrations.

(a) What is the independent variable?
(b) What is the dependent variable?
(c) What is the predicted relationship between the independent and dependent variables?
(d) What is the null hypothesis?

(Answers on p. 149)

Assuming that we have shown that the reading scheme has some effect, you will remember that a further question raised by the 'sceptic' teacher was whether it is children who are good or poor spellers who are most likely to benefit from the reading scheme.

One way of investigating this would be to vary spelling ability as an independent variable. The researcher might give all the children a spelling test and select two groups of children, one group consisting of top spellers and the other group poorer spellers. If both groups were given the reading scheme it would be possible to see what effect the independent variable of spelling ability has on the other variable of reading scores. In other words, was it the group of good spellers or the group of poor spellers who showed most improvement in reading scores?

One point you may have noticed is that it is not possible for an experimenter to 'manipulate' an independent variable like spelling ability in quite the same way as deciding whether to give children a reading scheme or not. In this latter case, it is entirely up to the researcher to decide which children to put in the reading-scheme group and which children to put in the no-reading-scheme group. With spelling ability, there is no way an experimenter can *make* a child into a good or bad speller. Nevertheless, by selecting groups of good and bad spellers, the researcher can manipulate the variable of spelling ability by setting up two experimental groups: high spelling ability and low spelling ability. The experimental hypothesis might be that only good spellers would show improvement from the reading scheme. In other words, the researcher would be predicting a *difference* between the reading scores of the two groups of children after they had been exposed to the reading scheme.

Another example of this kind of independent variable is sex. Even the most omnipotent experimenter cannot transform men into women or vice versa. Yet it is very common to select groups of men and women in order to investigate whether the variable of sex results in differences in performance on various tasks.

1.3   CORRELATIONAL DESIGNS

There are times, however, when experimenters are less interested in predicting differences in behaviour as a result of an independent variable. Instead they want to investigate whether variables are *associated* together. Take again the relationship between the variables of spelling ability and reading scores. A researcher might predict that over the *whole range* of spelling ability and reading ability children who are good spellers will also tend to score highly on a reading test, while children at the bottom end of the spelling scale will not do so well at reading. This might be important if you wanted to use a spelling test to pick out potential good readers.

Once again all the children would be given a spelling test and a reading test. But this time *neither* of the variables will be the independent or the dependent variable. The researcher will take measures of both variables in order to see whether those children who score highly on spelling also score highly on a reading test, while children who score less well on spelling also score less well on the reading test. This is known as a *correlational design*, the object of which is to test the experimental hypothesis that children's performance on the spelling ability variable *correlates* with their performance on the reading test variable.

There is one point you should notice about a correlational design. Because neither of the variables are being manipulated by the experimenter, it is not possible to predict which variable is having an effect on the other variable. All one can say is that there is a relationship between the two variables. For instance, it would be possible to give plausible arguments in favour of quite different relationships between spelling ability and the likelihood of benefiting from a reading scheme.

(1) Children who are good at spelling are likely to benefit from a reading scheme.
(2) Doing well as a result of a reading scheme itself improves children's spelling.
(3) Both good spelling and benefiting from reading schemes are the result of some other variable altogether, e.g. a positive attitude by parents towards school lessons.

It is because of this uncertainty that experimenters like to be able to manipulate independent variables whenever they can. However, there are many occasions when, although it might be possible to manipulate a variable, it is not ethical to do so.

Question 2

Suppose that a correlation has been demonstrated between smoking and lung cancer.

(a) Suggest three possible explanations for this correlation (like the ones for the correlation between spelling and reading improvement scores).

(b) Would it be possible to manipulate one of the variables as an independent variable? If so, would it be ethical?

(Answers on p. 149)

Both correlational designs and experiments in which variables are manipulated are useful in psychological research and there are appropriate statistical tests for each kind of experiment. The next chapters will be concerned with experiments in which variables are manipulated in order to test predicted *differences* in performance under different experimental conditions. However, we shall come back to correlational designs and statistical tests in Chapter 9.

If you are particularly interested in correlational designs you can, of course, turn directly to Chapter 9. However, you will need to read Chapters 3 and 4 first in order to understand the principles underlying the use and interpretation of statistical tests.

PROGRESS BOX ONE

1 An *experimental hypothesis* predicts a relationship between variables.

2 *Variables* are any characteristics which vary in an experimental situation.

3 In one type of experimental design the experimenter manipulates *independent variables* and predicts their effects on *dependent variables*.

4 The experimenter sets up *experimental conditions* in which an independent variable is varied (e.g. reading scheme versus no reading scheme). The data resulting from this type of experiment are *differences* in the dependent variable (e.g. reading scores) between the people allocated to the experimental conditions.

5 Another type of design known as a *correlational design* predicts a relationship between two variables, neither of which is manipulated by the experimenter (e.g. spelling scores and reading scores). The data resulting from this type of experiment are the two sets of related scores.

6 The *null hypothesis* states that the data resulting from an experiment are *not* due to the effects of an independent variable or a correlation between two variables as predicted by the experimental hypothesis. Instead they are chance fluctuations in people's performance due to the effects of other unknown variables.

CHAPTER 2

Experimental Designs

You may be wondering by now what all this talk about experiments has to do with statistics—which is, after all, the whole purpose of this book. The point is that the kinds of statistical tests used in psychology only make sense if you are aware of their role in evaluating experimental data. As the sceptic says to the researcher, 'How can you be certain that the improvement in reading scores that you attribute to your reading scheme is big enough to count as a real difference between the reading scheme group and the no reading scheme group? Perhaps the results of your experiment were all due to chance fluctuations in performance.'

And the researcher replies, 'Ah well, I went off and did a statistical test which told me that the difference in reading scores between the two groups was unlikely to have occurred simply by chance. It was a big enough and a consistent enough difference to count as a real difference between the two groups of children.'

The basic aim is to test whether any differences predicted by the experimental hypothesis *are* significant; or whether a researcher should instead accept the null hypothesis that such differences are only due to chance fluctuations in people's performance.

Unfortunately, there is no one all-purpose statistical test which can be used to test the results from all experimental designs. Which statistical test is suitable depends on the number of experimental conditions, how many variables are being manipulated and what kind of measurement is used for measuring a dependent variable like reading scores. The remaining sections of this chapter will describe those aspects of experimental designs which are relevant to selecting an appropriate statistical test.

2.1 EXPERIMENTAL DESIGNS WITH ONE INDEPENDENT VARIABLE

Let us start by reminding you that, in order to test a predicted relationship between an independent variable and a dependent variable, the experimenter has to set up *experimental conditions* in order to compare the performance of the people (*subjects*) who are allocated to one condition or another.

We shall now take you through some experimental designs, starting with the simplest case in which the experimenter simply wants to see whether an independent variable has any effect on people's performance.

2.1.1   Experimental and Control Conditions

Take again the example of investigating the effect of a reading scheme on children's reading scores. Suppose a researcher has an experimental hypothesis which predicts that a reading scheme will improve children's reading scores.

Do you think it would be a sufficient test of this hypothesis to give a group of children the reading scheme, and then to measure their reading scores?

How would the researcher know whether the children's reading scores were any higher than they would have been if they had been given no reading scheme at all? One way of dealing with this is to give the children a reading test *before* the reading scheme and then another test *afterwards* to see whether their scores had improved. The experimental design would look like this:

Test 1	*Experimental condition*	*Test* 2
Pre-test of reading scores	Reading scheme	Post-test of reading scores

Suppose the researcher found that the children's reading scores were indeed higher on the post-test than on the pre-test. Could he or she be sure that the improvement in reading scores from pre-test to post-test was caused by the reading scheme?

Even if there were an improvement in scores it might have occurred in any case, either because the children were that much older, or because of all the other changes which might have happened to them between the two tests, e.g. a new teacher had arrived, and it was this change that had increased their reading scores. The only way to discover whether any improvement in scores is due to the independent variable of the reading scheme is to design an experiment in which the *only* difference between conditions is whether children have been given the reading scheme or not.

It is for this reason that experimental designs introduce a *control* condition against which the effects of an independent variable can be compared. The point about a control condition is that it is a condition in which people are *not* subjected to the independent variable. So it is possible to compare two conditions, one *with* the independent variable (reading scheme) and one *without* the independent variable (no reading scheme). The experimental design would be

Experimental condition
   Pre-test scores   Reading scheme   Post-test scores
Control condition
   Pre-test scores   No reading scheme   Post-test scores

The prediction would be that there would be more improvement in the post-test reading scores for the experimental condition than for the control condition. With this design the researcher might indeed find some improvement in scores for both conditions due to other variables such as growing older or new teachers. However, if there were a significantly *greater* improvement in the experimental condition, it can be claimed that this extra improvement is due, not to natural changes which might have affected both conditions equally, but to the reading scheme which affected only the experimental condition and not the control condition.

Sometimes, rather than comparing an experimental and a control condition, it is more appropriate to compare two levels of an independent variable. An example would be an experiment to investigate whether lists of common words are easier to remember than lists of rare words. The experimental design would simply compare memory scores under two experimental conditions:

Experimental condition 1
   Learning lists of common words
Experimental condition 2
   Learning lists of rare words

2.1.2   Three or More Experimental Conditions

So far we have been talking about comparing only *two* experimental conditions. But you might want to look at more than two levels of an independent variable. For instance, you might be interested in whether different reading schemes would have different effects on children's reading scores. So you might like to compare the effects of reading scheme A and reading scheme B. You would still probably feel that it would be a good idea to have a control condition with no reading scheme. So the experimental design would have *three* conditions as follows:

Experimental condition 1
   Pre-test scores   Reading scheme A   Post-test scores
Experimental condition 2
   Pre-test scores   Reading scheme B   Post-test scores
Control condition
   Pre-test scores   No reading scheme   Post-test scores

This would still count as manipulating *one* independent variable (reading schemes) but that independent variable would have *three* conditions (two experimental conditions and one control condition). The prediction would be that there will be differences in scores between the three conditions.

Rather than just looking at overall differences between the three conditions, you might want to predict that the effect of the three levels would show a *trend*, with least improvement in the no reading scheme condition, an intermediate amount of improvement for reading scheme B and most improvement for reading scheme A.

Another example might be an experiment with *three* experimental conditions, for instance, learning lists of very common words, less common words and words which occur very rarely.

Question 3

(a) What would be the three experimental conditions for this experiment?
(b) What kind of trend might the experimenter predict between memory scores for the three experimental conditions?

2.2 EXPERIMENTAL DESIGNS WITH TWO OR MORE INDEPENDENT VARIABLES

In the kinds of experiment we have discussed so far, the experimenter is looking at the effects of *one* independent variable, e.g. reading scheme versus no reading scheme. But it is often the case that a particular variable may have one effect on people's behaviour in one situation and quite another effect in another situation. An example is two schemes for teaching children to read. With backward readers, reading scheme A might be much better at improving reading scores; but with more advanced readers, it might be reading scheme B which causes a greater improvement in reading scores. In order to see whether there is an *interaction* of this kind between initial reading ability and which reading scheme is most helpful, it is necessary to design an experiment in which *both* of the variables (reading ability *and* type of reading scheme) can be looked at *in one and the same experiment*.

2.2.1 Two-by-Two Designs

Let us take the case of an experiment which is designed to investigate the kinds of processes involved in understanding written texts. Suppose a researcher wanted to test the following experimental hypothesis: on a quick read through, a text consisting of short simple unconnected sentences will be easier to remember; however, if a person is given a longer time to study, then they will remember more of a text consisting of complex longer sentences which make the text more coherent.

Groups of subjects are given either passage A (simple sentences) or passage B (complex sentences) and are allowed to study the texts for either 2 or 10 min. From this you can see that the experimenter is manipulating *two* independent variables: the type of text (passage A or passage B) *and* the amount of time for studying the texts (2 or 10 min).

The experimenter may not be particularly interested in the effect or either variable on its own. It might be quite interesting to see whether passage A or passage B is easier to remember regardless of how much study time is allowed. With the study time variable, it is fairly obvious that 10 min study time will produce better recall than 2 min study time. The real point of the experiment is to see whether these two variables interact. Does allowing more or less study time have an effect on which type of text is easier to remember?

What experimental conditions would be needed in order to look at the effects of *two* independent variables? To investigate the effects of two types of text (passage A: simple sentences or passage B: complex sentences) and two amounts of study time (2 or 10 min), four experimental conditions would be necessary as follows:

Condition 1
  2 min study time for passage A
Condition 2
  10 min study time for passage A
Condition 3
  2 min study time for passage B
Condition 4
  10 min study time for passage B

Check for yourself that this means that every combination of study time and text passage has been allocated to one of the four conditions.

Another way of presenting these four conditions for the two variables is in a 2 × 2 table (Table 1).

Table 1 2 × 2 Table

	Study time variable	
Type of text variable	*Short study* (2 *min*)	*Long study* (10 *min*)
Passage A (simple sentences)		
Passage B (complex sentences)		

Question 4

To test whether you understand this, write in Table 1 which of the conditions 1 to 4 listed above fit into each square.

The next step is to imagine that the dependent variable, i.e. subjects' memory for texts, has been measured by the number of ideas correctly recalled. These recall scores for the four conditions have been inserted in the appropriate column in Table 2 (the actual scores are not meant to be realistic—simply an example for this particular design).

Table 2 Recall scores (number of ideas recalled)

	Study time variable		
Type of text variable	Short study (2 min)	Long study (10 min)	Total
Passage A (simple sentences)	10	6	16
Passage B (complex sentences)	1	12	13
Total	11	18	

We can now look at the table to see whether there are any differences in recall scores due to the experimenter's manipulation of the variables of study time and text passages. Although there are four conditions, it is possible to look at the effects of the two independent variables separately. We can do this by looking at the total scores for the rows and the columns in Table 2.

The total recall scores for the rows (16 and 13) represent memory scores for the two text passages, regardless of study time. This is the *main effect* of the sentence structure variable, somewhat more ideas being recalled from passage A than from passage B.

The total recall scores for the columns (11 and 18) represent memory scores for the two study times, regardless of which passage is being studied. This is the *main effect* of study time, more ideas being recalled with 10 min study time than with 2 min study time.

There is also an *interaction* between the two variables. When only 2 min study time is allowed, more ideas are recalled from passage A than from passage B (10 against 1). But when 10 min study time is allowed, more ideas are recalled from passage B (12 against 6).

Question 5

Do the recall scores in Table 2 support or go against the experimental hypothesis about length of study time and the sentence structure of text passages?

Question 6

(a) Draw a 2 × 2 table for an experiment investigating the effects of two reading schemes for teaching backward and more advanced readers. *Hint*: One variable would be the two reading schemes and the other would be whether children are backward or advanced readers.
(b) What would be the four experimental conditions?
(c) Allocate the four conditions to the columns in the 2 × 2 table as in the answer to Question 4.

2.2.2   Extensions of 2 × 2 Designs

In the preceding section we considered 2 × 2 designs. In these there are two independent variables, each testing two conditions of each variable. In the memory experiment the two variables were the sentence structure of text passages and length of study time. There were two conditions for each: complex and simple sentences and short and long study time. However, it is possible to look at any number of variables, each with any number of conditions.

Let us take a case where we are still looking at only two variables but one of them has three conditions. An example would be if we looked at *three* types of texts: simple, intermediate and complex and measured recall after a short or long study time. This would be termed a 2 × 3 design because there would still be *two* levels of the study time variable but *three* levels of the sentence structure variable.

How would you set about deciding how many experimental conditions you would need in order to test all possible main effects and interactions between these variables? There is a simple rule of thumb that the number of experimental conditions needed to test all possible combinations of the two variables for a 2 × 3 design is 2 × 3 = 6. Such a design would result in a 2 × 3 table as shown in Table 3. Of course, it does not matter whether you think of this as a 2 × 3 design (with the study time conditions at the top and the types of text conditions along the rows) or as a 3 × 2 design (with the conditions the other way round).

Table 3   2 × 3 Table

Type of text variable	*Study time variable*	
	Short study	*Long study*
Simple sentences	Condition 1	Condition 2
Intermediate sentences	Condition 3	Condition 4
Complex sentences	Condition 4	Condition 6

Designs of this kind can be extended: for example, two variables each with three conditions (3 × 3); *three* variables each with two conditions (2 × 2 × 2), and so on. The principles behind them are all exactly the same. In each case, experimental conditions are chosen to text every possible combination of the variables. On the basis of the scores in each condition, we can assess the main effects of each variable in isolation and also their interactions with all the other variables.

Question 7

How many experimental conditions would you need for a 3 × 3 design with *three* conditions of simple, intermediate and complex sentences and *three* conditions of short, medium and long study time?

PROGRESS BOX TWO

1 In experiments in which *one* independent variable is being manipulated, its effect is never assessed in isolation. It is compared either with a *control* condition (presence of the independent variable as opposed to absence of the independent variable) or with other experimental conditions. In other words, predictions about the effects of the independent variable state that *differences* will be found between conditions: either between an experimental and a control condition or between two or more experimental conditions.

2 In experiments in which *two or more* independent variables are being manipulated, experimental conditions are allocated so that it is possible to make comparisons between the *main effects* of each independent variable separately, and also to look at *interactions* between the variables.

3 In all cases, if differences in performance are found *between* conditions, this is interpreted as evidence in support of the experimental hypothesis. If there are only chance differences in subjects' scores then the experimental hypothesis has not been supported and instead the null hypothesis must be accepted.

2.3   RELATED AND UNRELATED DESIGNS

Until now we have implied that different groups of people would be allocated to different experimental conditions. But this is not always the case, since sometimes the same people are used for all experimental conditions.

2.3.1   Different Subjects

There are many experiments when it is essential to use different people for each experimental condition. Think again about the research into reading schemes.

Do you think it would be sensible to use different *children for the groups being given the reading scheme or no reading scheme? Or might the* same *children be used in both groups?*

You can imagine how difficult it would be for a single group of children to undergo both conditions. The only possibility would be for them all to be given the no reading scheme condition *first* and the reading scheme condition *second*. But then one would be back in the situation of not knowing whether any reading improvement was due to the reading scheme or to the fact that the children were older on the second occasion. We hope you can see that there would be even more problems about interpreting the results if the children had the reading scheme first and no reading scheme second. Even supposing that there was an improvement after the reading scheme, what could one really conclude if there was further improvement during a subsequent no-reading-scheme period?

Imagine, too, that you were interested in whether boys or girls were more likely to benefit from the reading scheme. There is simply no way (apart from a split-second sex change) in which the same children could be allocated to both the boys and girls groups. So there would obviously have to be different people in the two groups. The same would apply if you wanted to look at differences between good and bad spellers. At any given moment people are either good or bad at spelling and so *different* people would have to be allocated to the good and bad spelling groups.

This kind of experimental design is known as a *between-subjects* or *unrelated* design, because the comparison is *between* two groups of subjects whose scores are *unrelated*.

There are other cases when it is easier to use different subjects. For instance, there are experiments which may depend on, at least temporarily, misleading people about the true purpose of the experiment. To take an example, people may be asked to look at a list of words and put them into certain categories. Then they are suddenly asked to remember the words when they were not expecting to. This kind of experiment depends on subjects not knowing about the memory task beforehand. You could not use the same people more than once because the second time round they would already know that you were going to spring a 'surprise' memory task on them.

So far we have been talking about the need to use different people rather than the same people for all experimental conditions. But there is one crucial *disadvantage* about using different subjects to do different experimental conditions. This is that there may be all sorts of individual differences in the way different subjects tackle the experimental task.

For instance, in a reading experiment some people might think the experiment a bore, some might not even be able to read, some might be old, some young, some might be planning their next holiday, and others might have forgotten their spectacles. Such variability might affect their ability to read a text, from nil by a person who cannot read to 100% by an ambitious person who thinks he is going to get an A grade for his performance. As a result of all these individual differences people's performance might be affected by irrelevant variables which have nothing to do with the independent variable the experimenter is intending to manipulate. The danger is that all the people who are likely to do well on memory tasks might happen to be allocated to one experimental condition, e.g. reading a text with simple sentences. This would mean that memory scores for this condition would be artifically inflated, solely because of irrelevant variables that have nothing to do with the independent variable of simple versus complex sentences.

For this reason it is usual to allocate different people at *random* to experimental conditions. Here *random* means that it is purely a matter of *chance* which people end up doing which condition. The reasoning is that, if subjects are randomly allocated to experimental conditions on a chance basis, then people of different ages or abilities are just as likely to be found in all the experimental groups. For example, you might find that all the subjects who arrive first to volunteer for an experiment are the most highly motivated people who tend to score more highly, quite regardless of experimental condition. So they should not be placed in the same group. It would be better to allocate alternate subjects as they arrived, or perhaps to toss a coin to decide which group each subject should be allocated to; in which case—unless your coin is biased—the allocation of subjects to groups should be truly random.

2.3.2 Same Subjects

From the point of view of eliminating individual differences, there is, however, an even better experimental design than random allocation of different subjects. This is to use the *same* subjects for all experimental conditions. The point is that anything peculiar to one individual (like high or low motivation) is spread across all conditions. If a person is highly motivated when reading one text, thus inflating the scores for that condition, he will also tend to be well motivated when reading other texts and so will inflate those scores as well. The point about using a same subjects design is that any individual pecularities get equalized out over all conditions.

This is known as a *within-subjects* or *related* design, because the comparison is *within* the same group of subjects, the scores from each subject being related.

Think back to the experiment investigating memory for text passages with simple or complex sentences. Can you think of any problems if the same people read both passages?

Clearly you would have to provide two text passages with *different* content. If both passage A and passage B were about the same topic, then subjects' memory of the second passage might be affected by their recall of the other passage. But it would also be necessary to try and *equalize* the content of the two passages, so that neither would be more striking or easier to remember.

Finally, you would want to vary the *order* in which subjects read the two passages. Otherwise they might remember the second passage better just because they had had some practice with the first passage. If all the subjects read passage A first and passage B second, they might do better on passage B for that reason only. It is in fact standard practice never to give subjects all the experimental conditions in the same order. For instance, with two conditions, half the subjects would be given passage A, then passage B; and the other half passage B followed by passage A. In this way any order effects can be *counterbalanced* between the two experimental conditions.

All this goes to show how many things have to be taken into account when designing an experiment. The point is to try and eliminate all possible irrelevant variables which might be affecting subjects' performance (such as the content of the texts, order of presentation, and so on). The only difference between the two conditions should be the difference between the simple sentences in passage A and the complex sentences in passage B.

The dilemma is that, if the experimenter decides to use the *same* subjects, then the text passages have to be carefully matched and presented in a counterbalanced order. On the other hand, if the experimenter uses *different* subjects, exactly the same text passages can be used for the two conditions. But with this design there is the problem that the two groups of subjects may vary in ways irrelevant to the purpose of the experiment.

2.3.3 Matched Subjects

One way out of this dilemma is to try and match the subjects doing each experimental condition (a *matched-subjects* design). The idea is to match sets of subjects on sex, age, reading ability, motivation, spelling ability and so on—depending on which characteristics seem important for a particular experiment.

Suppose, for instance, it is thought that the sex of children is relevant to their performance on a reading test. There are two possibilities. Either you can have different groups of boys and girls so as to investigate whether there is a difference. Alternatively, you can arrange to match up boys and girls so that there are equal numbers of boys and girls in each group. In this way neither group will have a preponderance of boys or girls and so performance will not be affected by this variable.

Another example might be the age of subjects. You might be investigating whether widows or widowers adjust better to their bereavement. But it might be the case that widows always tend to be older, or poorer, so that any differences in behaviour may be due to these variables rather than to any special differences between men and women. So you might decide to match for age (an irrelevant variable as far as the comparison between widows and widowers is concerned). The usual method is to select equal numbers of widows and widowers for each age, so that for each widow there is a widower of the same age. If these pairs are allocated to each group, you will end up with an equal range of ages in the widows and the widowers groups.

A matched-subjects design can be treated as a related design. This is because the aim is to match sets of subjects on all characteristics relevant to an experiment so that, for the purposes of that experiment, they are as nearly as possible the *same* people. In the case of a same-subjects related design, the subjects *are*, of course, the same people doing all the experimental conditions.

It may seem that matched-subjects designs do indeed combine all the virtues of using same subjects and different subjects. Because the groups consist of different people it is possible to use the same materials and there is no need to worry about order effects. Yet, because sets of matched subjects are allocated to experimental conditions, variability due to the characteristics of different subjects should be much lessened.

Unfortunately, matching subjects has problems of its own. Often it is just not possible to find subjects who are matched on all relevant character-istics. It would be rare indeed for an experimenter to know beforehand all the individual variables which are likely to have an effect on people's per-formance. Moreover, in the kinds of experiments you are likely to be doing, you will probably only have small numbers of people available to act as subjects in your experiments, often other students taking similar courses. It is only in large-scale research that it is possible to select groups of subjects who can be matched on important variables, such as age, social class, intelligence, reading ability and so on.

PROGRESS BOX THREE

Advantages and disadvantages of different subjects and same subjects:

	Advantages	*Disadvantages*
Between-subjects *unrelated* designs (i.e. *different* subjects doing experimental conditions)	1 Necessary for natural groups, e.g. different ages or sex 2 Necessary for experiments in which subjects are misled or taken by surprise 3 No order effects	1 The use of different subjects introduces individual differences which may affect performance (partially offset by allocating subjects randomly to groups)
Within-subjects *related* designs (i.e. *same* subjects doing experimental conditions)	1 Eliminates individual differences between experimental conditions	1 Cannot be used when subjects *have* to be different, e.g. men and women 2 Problem of counterbalancing order effects, content of experimental materials, etc.
Matched-pairs *related* designs (i.e. *different* but *matched* subjects doing experimental conditions)	1 Has the advantages listed under between-subjects designs because different people are doing the experimental conditions 2 Attempts to eliminate individual differences by using matched subjects who are likely to perform in the same way	1 Although this design attempts to combine the advantages of both within-subject and between-subject designs, one can never be sure that subjects are matched on all the variables which are likely to affect performance

In most psychological experiments it is *not* sufficient simply to allocate equal numbers of males and females to different experimental conditions and claim that you have matched your groups. In order to match subjects it is necessary to equalize all possible relevant variables, so that matched subjects can be treated for the purposes of the experiment as if they were indeed the 'same' person. In most cases, therefore, if you use different people for different experimental conditions, you should treat this as an *unrelated experimental design*.

Question 8

Can you think of any pairs of people who are naturally matched and so have often been used in experiments?

2.4 LEVELS OF MEASUREMENT

It is obviously a crucial matter to decide how you are going to measure the behaviour of your subjects. Having varied an independent variable, you have to obtain some measure of the dependent variable, e.g. improvement in reading scores or number of words recalled from a text passage.

It is generally considered essential for the measurement of the dependent variable to be *quantitative*; and *objective* in the sense that the measure will always give the same results regardless of who is doing the measuring. This insistence on quantitative, objective measurement does not necessarily mean that only rather uninteresting aspects of human behaviour can be studied. A quantitative measure might be of people's responses to a questionnaire about their innermost feelings; or it might be some measure of natural behaviour such as the number of people who will answer questions put to them by total strangers.

It is not always easy to use strictly numerical scores to measure behaviour. Imagine an experiment to test whether people who get a good grade in a course are more or less likely to re-register for another course. The independent variable is whether students get good or bad grades and the dependent variable is whether they re-register or not. The only method of measuring the dependent variable is to allocate the students into categories, in this case whether they re-register or not. This is called *nominal* measurement because it gives only a label, or *name*, to categories of people.

But, suppose that you want the students to rate courses they have taken as being very good, good, medium, bad or very bad. You are immediately introducing a relationship into the data, namely, better or worse. This is known as *ordinal* measurement because it involves a *rank ordering* or scores. One point to note about ordinal data is that it does *not* imply that there are *equal* intervals between the judgements of good, better, best, etc. You can be certain that 'very good' is 'better' than 'good' and that 'good' is 'better' than 'bad', i.e. you can put them in a rank order. But can you say that there is exactly the same gap or interval between 'very good' and 'good' as that between 'bad' and 'very bad'?

When it comes to numerical scores, such as numbers of items recalled or reading times, you are dealing with numbers and you can assume that the distances between scores *are* the same. This type of measurement is known as *interval* measurement because it assumes *equal intervals* between the data on a continuous numerical scale. It is assumed that remembering two items as opposed to three items represents the same interval as that between remembering three and four items. Consequently, you are allowed to perform *numerical operations* on this kind of data. This makes it possible to carry out more complex kinds of statistical analysis, which take advantage of the numerical relationships between the scores.

There is another kind of measurement, which is mentioned in most psychology statistical textbooks, *ratio* measurement. This involves the kind of numerical scale which has an absolute zero (e.g. where there is a genuine zero like nil length) as opposed to temperature (where $0°$ on a centigrade or Fahrenheit scale does not mean a nil temperature). However, you do not need to bother about the difference between interval and ratio scales. For the purpose of statistical analysis in psychology both measures are treated in exactly the same way.

But there is an important point to be borne in mind about the measurement of psychological variables. This is that it is very common for scales which are *ordinal*, such as a seven-point scale between very good and very bad, to be allotted numbers from 1 to 7 and then treated as if these represent *equal numerical intervals*. This is often perfectly justifiable. But you should always consider what a conversion from an ordinal scale to an interval scale implies and whether it is appropriate.

PROGRESS BOX FOUR

The four types of measurement can be summarized as follows:

Nominal	Allocates people into categories
Ordinal	Data which can be put into rank order
Interval	Data on a continuous numerical scale with equal intervals between points
Ratio	As interval, with an absolute zero

Question 9

Which kinds of measurement would be appropriate for measuring:

(a) Pass or failure on an exam?
(b) Teachers' ratings of educational aptitude?
(c) Children's scores on an arithmetic test ranging from 0 to 100%?

CHAPTER 3

Statistical Analysis

We now come back to the problem that however much you try to eliminate irrelevant variables in your experimental design you can never get rid of *all* the variability in people's behaviour. This variability in your subjects' performance will inevitably be reflected in whatever measure you take of the dependent variable. So what you will find yourself faced with is experimental data consisting of a whole range of different scores by subjects.

What you want to know is: are the differences in the scores the result of manipulating the independent variable? Or are there no real differences apart from chance fluctuations in people's performance due to unknown variables, as stated by the null hypothesis?

3.1 VARIABILITY OF SCORES

Let us take an example. Suppose your experimental hypothesis is that people will have better memory recall for simple texts than for complex texts. You vary the independent variable by giving one group of subjects a simple text to read and another group a complex text. You score numbers of ideas correctly recalled as a measure of the dependent variable. When you run the experiment with a number of subjects you end up with a collection of recall scores for the subjects in each condition.

If the subjects had all reacted in exactly the same way, so that they *all* got better recall scores for simple texts, you might feel pretty confident about saying that the experimental hypothesis had been supported. But, of course, people are not all the same. Their performance on a memory recall task will vary for all sorts of reasons that have nothing to do with the experimental prediction about simple and complex texts.

Imagine that, after running the experiment, you end up with recall scores for ten subjects in each condition as shown in Table 4. These recall scores represent the number of ideas correctly recalled by each subject. The first thing to do is to calculate the *average* recall scores for the two conditions (this average is known as the *mean* for each condition). To calculate the mean for Condition 1 add up the total number of ideas correct for all ten subjects. Then divide this total by 10 (the number of subjects in Condition 1) to get the mean for Condition 1. Do the same for the Condition 2 scores.

Table 4 Number of ideas correctly recalled
(out of 10)

Condition 1 (simple texts)	Condition 2 (complex texts)
10	2
5	1
6	3
3	4
9	4
8	4
7	2
5	5
6	7
5	4
Totals 64	36

Try calculating the means for Condition 1 and Condition 2 for yourself.

The mean for Condition 1 is $64 \div 10 = 6.4$. The mean for Condition 2 is $36 \div 10 = 3.6$. The difference between the means for Condition 1 and Condition 2 is 2.8. The question we now have to ask is whether this difference between the means is large enough to represent a *real* difference between Condition 1 and Condition 2 subjects when we take into account all the variability in scores.

There would be no problem if each and every subject in Condition 1 had recalled exactly 6.4 ideas while every one in Condition 2 had recalled 3.6 ideas. In that case it would be reasonable to claim that the subjects in Condition 1 scored more highly than those in Condition 2.

But life is not that easy. In fact the means represent numerical averages around which there is quite a wide spread or *range* of scores in each condition. For instance, in Condition 1 the scores range from as little as 3 to as many as 10 out of 10.

What is the range of scores in Condition 2?

As you can see from Table 4, scores in Condition 2 range from 1 to 7 ideas recalled. In other words, there is a considerable amount of variability in scores around the mean even for subjects who are doing exactly the same experimental condition.

How can we measure the amount of variability in scores around a mean? Let us start by calculating the mean for all the scores shown in Table 4. The mean for all the scores in the table is the grand total of all scores ($64 + 36$) divided by the total number of subjects (20), which works out at a mean of 5 ideas correctly recalled.

The best way to look at *total variability* is to plot all the subjects' recall scores in a *histogram* like that shown in Figure 1. The histogram shows number of correctly recalled ideas along the bottom, i.e. all possible scores from 0 to 10 ideas correct. The number of subjects who got each score are shown up the vertical axis (each square representing a person). We have used all twenty subjects regardless of which experimental condition they were in. The resulting histogram shows the *total distribution* of recall scores obtained by all the subjects. For each subject, there is a square which represents his or her particular recall score.

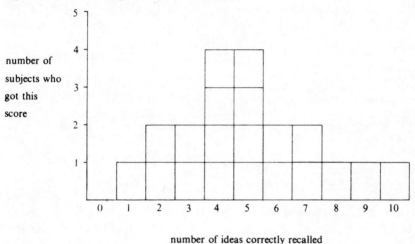

number of ideas correctly recalled

Figure 1

Question 10

(a) How many subjects scored 5 correct ideas?
(b) Did more subjects score 4 or 7 correct?
(c) Did any subject recall no ideas correctly?
(d) Did any subject recall all the ideas correctly?
(e) How many subjects were there altogether?

It is obvious from the histogram in Figure 1 that there is quite a lot of variability around the mean of 5 correct ideas correctly recalled. In fact, only 4 subjects got exactly this score while the other subjects achieved scores that ranged from 1 to 10 correct. Clearly the mean does not tell us everything we need to know about subjects' scores. We also need a measure of the variability of scores around that mean. As we will see in later chapters, this is done by calculating how much each individual score *deviates* from the mean.

The histogram in Figure 1 shows the total variability in all the subjects' scores. But what we are interested in is the *differences* between the recall scores of subjects in the two different experimental conditions. In Figure 2 the two sets of scores are set out separately. Check that these histograms represent the same recall scores as those shown in Table 4 and Figure 1.

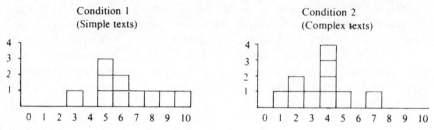

Figure 2

Question 11

(a) How many subjects in Condition 1 scored 5 correct ideas?
(b) How many subjects in Condition 2 scored 5 correct ideas?
(c) Did the Condition 1 or the Condition 2 subjects recall more ideas correctly?
(d) How many subjects in Condition 2 had a higher recall score than at least one person in Condition 1?

The histograms in Figure 2 demonstrate two points. You will remember that there is a relatively large difference between the *means* of the two conditions 6.4 ideas correct for Condition 1 as against 3.6 ideas correct for Condition 2. On the other hand, there is quite a lot of *variability* of scores around the mean in both conditions. You will notice that the variability is greater in Condition 1 with the scores spread out from 3 to 10, while the scores in Condition 2 are more bunched together. In both conditions, however, the mean represents not any particular score, but a numerical average around which the subjects' actual scores vary.

The fact that there is a difference between the means in the predicted direction appears to support the experimental hypothesis. But when we look at the variability in scores things are not so clear cut. What about the subject in Condition 1 who got only 3 ideas correct or the subject in Condition 2 who managed to get 7 out of 10 ideas correct. These results appear to go *against* the experimental hypothesis that more ideas will be recalled from simple texts.

How can you as a researcher decide whether any differences in scores are due to your manipulation of an independent variable, as predicted by the experimental hypothesis, or, alternatively, whether the differences are only due to chance fluctuations in performance, as stated by the null hypothesis? This is a real problem for psychologists because most of the data from psychological experiments is of this kind: differences in *means* between conditions, combined with a lot of *variability* in individual subjects' scores.

The whole point about statistical tests is that they can settle this question for you. Do the results from your experiment represent a *significant* difference in favour of the experimental hypothesis? If so, you are entitled to reject the null hypothesis that there are only chance differences due to unknown variables.

3.2   STATISTICAL PROBABILITIES

As we have just noted, with all the variability in subjects' scores, it would be rare indeed to find clear-cut 100% differences between the scores for different experimental conditions. So all a statistical test can provide is a *probability* that your results are significant.

The way this is done may seem rather paradoxical. The probabilities provided by statistical tests refer to probabilities that any differences in scores *are* due to chance fluctuations caused by unknown variables. This means that the *less* probable it is that any differences are due to chance fluctuations, the *more* confident you can be that there is a real significant difference due to your manipulation of the independent variable.

This is the *basis of all statistical tests of significance.* Statistical tests tell you the probability of getting the differences in scores found in your experiment if scores were in fact occurring on a chance basis. If this chance probability is very *low*, then you can *reject* the null hypothesis that the differences are chance differences. Instead you can accept the experimental hypothesis that your experimental results are significant, i.e. that they are *not* likely to have been chance effects.

Statistical tables provide a *distribution* of all the probabilities of experimental scores occurring by chance. This enables you to look up the exact percentage probability of getting your own results by chance. On this basis you can decide whether a very small percentage probability (say only 1%) that your results are chance results is low enough to entitle you to reject the null hypothesis, and accept your result as a *significant* difference in favour of the experimental hypothesis.

One important point we should emphasize here is that when we are talking about whether an experimental result is *significant*, there is always a specific percentage probability that *every* experimental result is a chance result. To get this idea across, suppose you tossed a coin a thousand times and got heads every time. You would probably think that the coin was definitely biased towards heads. However, there is a tiny probability that a run of a thousand heads in a row could occur even with an unbiased coin. However, because the probability of this happening is so small, you would be likely to accept that the coin *is* biased.

It is just the same with experimental results. A big difference in scores between conditions is probably due to the predicted effects of the independent variable rather than being just a chance difference. But there is always a small probability that it really is a chance result. So there can never be a 100% certainty that the results of your experiment were due to the effects of manipulating the independent variable as predicted by the experimental hypothesis. The most you can say is that the probability of your result having occurred by chance is so tiny that you are prepared to take the risk of rejecting the null hypothesis and accepting that there is a real significant difference between the experimental conditions.

3.3 SELECTING A LEVEL OF SIGNIFICANCE

So far we have not really tackled the question of why you would be prepared to accept one level of probability rather than another when deciding whether or not to reject the null hypothesis. What risk would you be prepared to accept that the scores resulting from your experiment occurred by chance, as stated by the null hypothesis, and were not significant at all? Of course, you would like to be 100% certain that the difference in scores is significant. But, as we said earlier, you can never be 100% certain that it is not a freak chance occurrence. Would you accept a 99% probability that your result is significant against a 1% probability that it is due to chance (i.e. a 1 in 100 chance that it is a chance result)? Or would you accept a 95% probability of significance against a 5% probability that it is chance (i.e. a 1 in 20 probability that it is a chance result)?

There is no simple answer. It is up to you to decide what odds you are prepared to accept when deciding whether the results of your experiment are significant. And for this reason an experimenter always has to state the odds which are being used to accept or reject the null hypothesis.

Imagine that you are investigating whether a new reading scheme might help backward children and you carried out an experiment in which you compared the progress of a group of children using your new scheme against a control group using traditional methods. Suppose you found a difference in reading improvement scores between the two groups in favour of the new scheme. Suppose the probability that this difference could have occurred by chance was 5% (i.e. 5 in 100 or a 1 in 20 probability that there were only chance differences rather than a significant difference caused by the reading scheme). Would you accept that the difference was significant and introduce the new reading scheme, and at what cost in materials and teacher training? Imagine another case where you are testing a powerful drug with nasty side effects and find an improvement in patients taking the drug as compared with a control group. If the difference between the groups could have occurred by chance 5 in 100 times, would you accept that the difference is significant and introduce the new drug? Would you change your odds if you knew that without the drug most of the patients would die anyway? And how would you feel if an aeroplane you were going to fly in had a 5% probability of developing electrical failure?

These examples bring home the fact that *choosing a significance level* is always a matter of deciding what odds you are prepared to accept that your results are due to chance. In the case of the reading scheme no one would probably suffer all that much if it was all due to chance after all; as long as it was not too expensive, you would probably go ahead and introduce the new scheme.

On the other hand, you might feel more doubtful about introducing a powerful drug with nasty side effects if there was a 1 in 20 probability that it was doing no good at all; although you might accept these odds if it were the only hope of saving people's lives. I don't think any of us would fly in a plane with a 1 in 20 chance of crashing.

In psychology (possibly because it is thought that nothing too terrible can happen as a result of accepting a result as significant!) it is a convention to accept odds of either 1 in 100 (i.e. 1%) or 5 in 100 (i.e. 5%) as grounds for rejecting the null hypothesis and instead accepting that the experimental hypothesis has been supported. The way this is expressed is to state that the probability of a result being due to chance is less than 1% or less than 5%. That is why in articles in psychological journals you will see statements that differences between experimental conditions were significant ($p < .01$); or ($p < .05$). This means that the probability (p) of a result occurring by chance is less than (expressed as $<$) 1% (.01) or 5% (.05). Sometimes you will find other probabilities quoted such as $p < .02$ or $p < .001$. These represent probabilities of obtaining a chance result of only 2 times in 100 and 1 in 1000 (2% and .1%). Clearly these give you even greater grounds for *rejecting* the null hypothesis that your results are due to the chance effects of unknown variables.

Question 12

Suppose that an experimenter reports that a significant difference has been found between subjects' recall scores for simple and complex texts $p < .001$.

(a) Which, if any, of the following are correct? The null hypothesis can be rejected because the probability of the difference being due to chance fluctuations is less than:

1 in 100 (1%),   1 in 20 (5%),   1 in 1000 (.1%).

(b) Which of the above would indicate the greatest level of significance?

To summarize, the whole aim of statistical tests is to tell you the percentage probability that your own results are chance differences rather than a significant effect due to the predicted effects of the independent variables. You can then see whether the percentage probability of a chance result is *lower* than the conventionally accepted levels of significance, 5% ($p < .05$) or 1% ($p < .01$).

Statistical tables provide a list of such percentage probabilities. To use these tables the first thing you will have to do is calculate the value of an appropriate 'statistic' for the statistical test you are applying. The step-by-step procedures in Chapters 6, 8 and 9 will tell you how to do this. You will also be instructed how to look up, in the appropriate statistical table, the value of the 'statistic' calculated from your own data to find its chance probability.

PROGRESS BOX FIVE

1 Subjects' scores in different experimental conditions vary around the mean.

2 Variability in scores will be due both to independent variables manipulated by the experimenter *and* to chance fluctuations in performance due to unknown variables irrelevant to the experimental hypothesis.

3 Statistical tests give percentage probabilities that the data from an experiment represent chance fluctuations due to unknown variables, as stated by the null hypothesis.

4 If this percentage probability is *below* a certain level—normally 1% ($p < .01$) or 5% ($p < .05$)—the experimenter can reject the null hypothesis and accept instead the experimental hypothesis that there are *significant* differences in scores due to the manipulation of independent variables.

CHAPTER 4

Selecting a Statistical Test

Now we come to the all important chapter as far as your ability to use statistical tests is concerned. As we pointed out earlier, it is necessary to choose an appropriate statistical test for each type of experimental design. In other words, the whole art of using psychological statistics is to match up the experimental designs described in Chapter 2 with the statistical tests listed in the remaining chapters of this book.

The reason for this is that the calculation of percentage probabilities of obtaining a chance result is based on the amount of variability in subjects' scores. The point was made in Chapter 2 that certain decisions about experimental designs, like deciding whether to use same or different subjects, will affect variability in the experimental data. Other relevant dimensions are how many experimental conditions are being manipulated in order to test one or more independent variables and how accurately your measure of the dependent variable reflects the variability in subjects' scores. Since each statistical test is based on a particular distribution of percentage probabilities, different statistical tests will be appropriate for experimental designs which allow for different amounts of variability.

So the first and most important point we want to emphasize is this: *the selection of an appropriate statistical test follows from the experimental design you have chosen to test your experimental hypothesis.* In fact, choice of a suitable test depends on a *very few* decisions about experimental design. Once you have made these decisions you will find that you have automatically selected which statistical test to use for analysing the significance of your experimental data. These decisions are summarized on the inside covers of this book.

In the next section we shall go through the main decisions about experimental designs. If you have forgotten about any of these designs, you may find it helpful to look back to the indicated sections in earlier chapters.

4.1   DECISIONS ABOUT EXPERIMENTAL DESIGNS

Some statistical tests are appropriate for testing *differences* in scores between experimental conditions (Chapter 1, Section 1.2). Other tests are suitable for testing whether two sets of scores are *correlated* (Chapter 1, Section 1.3).

Given that you are looking at *differences* between experimental conditions, different statistical tests need to be used depending on whether you are investigating *one independent variable* or *two or more independent variables.*

Also important is the *number of experimental conditions* in your experiment.

Your experiment might be designed to look at *differences* in scores between *two* experimental conditions as a result of manipulating *one* independent variable (Chapter 2, Section 2.1.1).

Your experiment might be designed to look at *differences* in scores or a *trend* in scores between *three or more* experimental conditions as a result of manipulating *one* independent variable (Chapter 2, Section 2.1.2).

Your experiment might be designed to look at *differences* in scores between *four or more* experimental conditions as a result of manipulating *two or more* independent variables (Chapter 2, Section 2.2).

Different statistical tests need to be used for analysing the significance of experimental data depending on whether it has been produced by the *same* or by *different* subjects doing the experimental conditions (Chapter 2, Section 2.3).

Finally, there are two main kinds of statistical tests, known as non-parametric and parametric tests. The distinction between the tests will be discussed fully in Chapter 7. However, one consideration when selecting between statistical tests is *level of measurement*, i.e. whether your data is measured on a *nominal, ordinal* or *interval* scale (Chapter 2, Section 2.4).

4.2   USING THE DECISION CHART

The Decision Chart on the inside covers incorporates all the decisions about experimental designs which are relevant for choosing an appropriate statistical test.

The way to use the chart is to start at the top and ask yourself the questions in the diamond-shaped boxes. Depending on your answer to each question, you should follow the line down to the next diamond-shaped box and answer that question.

Eventually you will reach an oblong-shaped box which gives the name of a statistical test. Sometimes there is more than one test in a box. This reflects the fact that for many kinds of experimental design there are parallel non-parametric tests and parametric tests, both of which are appropriate for that design. Which you should use to analyse your data depends partly on the level of measurement of your data and partly on other considerations which will be discussed in Chapter 7, Sections 7.4 and 7.5.

For the moment you won't have to bother about this distinction at all. Chapter 5 introduces only the simpler non-parametric tests. We would strongly recommend you to make yourself thoroughly familiar with the rationale and methods for calculating these tests, given in Chapter 6, before going on to tackle the parametric tests in Chapter 8.

It may also help you to identify the statistical test you ought to choose if you look at the beginning of the chapters in which the different kinds of tests are described. At the beginning of Chapter 6 there is a table showing the designs for which you should select appropriate *non-parametric* tests. At the beginning of Chapter 8 there is a table showing the correct selection of *parametric* tests. And at the beginning of Chapter 9 the conditions for using *correlational* tests are given.

4.3 LOOKING UP PROBABILITIES IN STATISTICAL TABLES

Whichever type of statistical test you use, you will end up by having to look up percentage probabilities in the statistical table appropriate for that particular test. This can, in fact, be quite confusing. Despite the fact that all the tables give exactly the same information about percentage probabilities, the way in which these are laid out differs from table to table.

To help you find your way through these difficulties, a few general tips are given in this chapter. You should not worry too much about these now, but you will find that they will help to explain why you do certain things when looking up a statistical table.

4.3.1 Degrees of Freedom

You will find that, when looking up statistical tables, you will have to take into account the total number of subjects in your experiment and/or the number of subjects in each experimental condition. This is because the chances of getting a big difference in scores or a high correlation depends on how large a sample of subjects you have tested. Furthermore, for some tests you will find that you have to look up one statistical table for small numbers of subjects and another table when you have used more subjects. Often the number of experimental conditions in your experiment is also relevant for looking up probabilities in a statistical table.

Sometimes you will be asked to take into account not just the number of subjects (N) but the number of subjects minus one $(N - 1)$. Sometimes it will be the number of conditions minus one $(C - 1)$ which will be relevant. We shall give you an example to put this over intuitively.

Imagine that you are seating eight people round a table. When you have told seven people where to sit this means that the eighth person must sit on the only chair left. There is no 'freedom' about where the last person will sit, so we would say that, although there are eight people (N), there are only seven degrees of freedon $(N - 1)$. Convince yourself that this applies however many people you are trying to seat in the first place.

Now imagine that you are old-fashioned enough to be trying to seat four men and four women in alternate seats around the table. Once you have seated three men and three women, everyone would know where the last man and the last woman would have to sit. This is like the case where there are two groups of four subjects; for each group there would be only three degrees of freedom.

Now let us take an experimental example. Suppose you carry out an experiment and calculate the total of the scores. When copying out the scores later, you forget to include one of them, so that you end up with:

S_1	12
S_2	13
S_3	10
S_4	11
S_5	14
S_6	blank
Total	75

You do not need to panic because you know that given five results and the total of all six results you can calculate the forgotten score. All you have to do is to subtract the five scores from the total; your sixth score could only have been 15.

Question 13

Suppose there are four conditions in an experiment and that the mean scores for each condition and for all subjects are as follows:

	Mean score
Condition 1 (four subjects)	8
Condition 2 (four subjects)	12
Condition 3 (four subjects)	20
Condition 4 (four subjects)	—
All subjects ($N = 16$)	16

Calculate the mean score for Condition 4. *Hint.* Calculate the totals for each condition and for all subjects by multiplying the mean score by the number of subjects.

The point about these two examples is that given the other scores and the total the missing score is completely predictable; in other words it cannot *vary*. It is just because of this 'lack of freedom' for one score to vary that degrees of freedom are calculated on the basis of those scores that *can* vary, that is, $N - 1$ or $C - 1$. Since all statistical texts are based on distributions of variability, degrees of freedom to vary needs to be taken into account when looking up statistical probabilities.

However, *you need not worry too much about this rather complex notion of degrees of freedom.* You will be told exactly what to do whenever degrees of freedom come up in connection with a statistical test.

4.3.2 One-tailed and Two-tailed Hypotheses

There is one further point about the way an experimental hypothesis is formulated which has implications for the way in which you look up probabilities in statistical tables. This is whether the experimental hypothesis is *unidirectional* (known as *one-tailed*) or *bidirectional* (known as *two-tailed*).

A unidirectional hypothesis is one that, as its name implies, makes a prediction in one particular direction. An example might be that short sentences will result in more ideas being remembered than long sentences. But there are other hypotheses which make a *bi*directional prediction by predicting that the effect of an independent variable may go in either direction. In our example, this would mean predicting that short sentences will result in either *more* ideas being remembered or *less* ideas being remembered, i.e. predicting that sentence length will have some effect but not being prepared to say what.

It is obviously preferable to be able to give an explanation of human behaviour in terms of predicting behaviour in one direction; rather than to state vaguely that there will be an effect of some kind in either direction. However, there are times, particularly during the more exploratory phase of a research programme, when you might just want to try out whether a variable has any effect; for example, whether a teaching method has any effect, good or bad, on children learning to read.

One-tailed and two-tailed hypotheses have implications for statistical analysis. The point is that for a hypothesis which predicts a difference in only *one* direction, there is a specific percentage probability that the difference might occur by chance. But, if a hypothesis makes a prediction that a difference might occur in *either* direction, then there is *double* the probability that such differences might occur by chance. There is the probability that a difference might occur in one direction *plus* the probability that a difference might occur in the other direction.

Imagine that the probability of getting a chance result in one direction is 1%. This means that you can reject the null hypothesis that it is a chance result at the $p < .01$ level of significance. But if your original prediction had been two-tailed in either direction, then there would be double the probability that it was a chance result, i.e. 2%. You would not be able to reject the null hypothesis at the 1% $(p < .01)$ level but only at the $(p < .02)$ level. In other words, with a two-tailed hypothesis there is a higher probability that it is a chance result.

You will find that some statistical tables give either one-tailed or two-tailed probabilities, not always both. Sometimes you will have to double the one-tailed probabilities for a two-tailed test, or halve the two-tailed probabilities for a one-tailed test, in order to arrive at the correct level of significance. You will be given detailed instructions about what to do for each test.

PROGRESS BOX SIX

All you need to know about statistical tests:

Before the experiment

1 Formulate your *experimental hypothesis* in terms of the predicted effects you expect to occur as a result of manipulating independent variables (Chapter 1).

2 By implication, the *null hypothesis* is that the results of your experiment will be due, not to the effects predicted by the experimental hypothesis, but to chance differences in scores due to other unknown variables (Chapter 1, Section 1.1).

3 Decide which is the appropriate statistical test for comparing your experimental results against the probability that they occurred by chance (Chapter 4, Section 4.1 and 4.2, and Decision Chart on inside covers).

After the experiment

4 Carry out the appropriate calculations on your experimental data (Chapters 6, 8 and 9).

5 Look up the appropriate statistical table in the Appendix (taking into account degrees of freedom and whether your experimental hypothesis is one-tailed or two-tailed) to see whether the probability of your result being a chance one is less than 5% $(p < .05)$ or 1% $(p < .01)$ (Chapter 4, Section 4.3).

6 On the basis of this decide whether you have to accept the null hypothesis that your results are due to chance, or whether you can reject the null hypothesis and interpret your results as supporting the experimental hypothesis (Chapter 3).

CHAPTER 5

Non-Parametric Tests: An Introduction

As was mentioned in the last chapter, there are two main kinds of statistical tests, known as parametric and non-parametric tests. The major difference between them is the sophistication of the measures used for calculating variability in scores.

We are going to introduce non-parametric tests first, mainly because they are much simpler to calculate. Rather than calculating exact numerical differences between scores, non-parametric tests only take into acount whether certain scores are higher or lower than other scores.

One important advantage of this is that non-parametric tests can be used when you can measure your experimental data only at the *ordinal* level; that is, when it is only capable of being ranked in order of magnitude. And there are some non-parametric tests which can be used even when your data is only *nominal*; that is, when subjects can only be allocated to categories (see Chapter 2, Section 2.4).

5.1 TESTS FOR RELATED AND UNRELATED DESIGNS

The major criterion for selecting an appropriate non-parametric test is based on whether you have used the *same* subjects for all experimental conditions or *different* groups of subjects for each condition. Chapter 2, Section 2.3 introduced you to certain considerations which might influence your decision on this matter and you may like to reread this now.

Why is this distinction between using same or different subjects so crucial for selecting an appropriate non-parametric test? The reason is that there are two sorts of comparisons that can be made between subjects' performance in different experimental conditions. If the *same* person does all experimental conditions, it is possible to make a direct comparison between that person's performance under the different conditions. With *matched* sets of subjects doing all the experimental conditions, it is also considered legitimate to make a direct comparison between the performance of these sets of subjects.

However, if *different* subjects are allocated to different experimental conditions, it should be obvious that there is no basis for making a direct comparison between any particular subject doing the first condition and any other particular subject doing the second condition. All that one can do is to make an *overall* comparison between the performance of the two groups.

It is for this reason that it is very important when presenting your experimental data in a table to indicate whether it was the same or different subjects who produced the scores for the different experimental conditions. From this point of view designs using matched subjects are treated as if they were same subjects. So in descriptions of statistical tests you can take it that 'same subjects' designs includes cases when you are using matched subjects (but see Chapter 2, Section 2.3.3, for some discussion about the problems of achieving a perfect matching of subjects).

Remember, too, that you should always include in your table of results the *mean scores* for each experimental condition. This is essential so that you can check whether any significant differences *are* in fact in the direction predicted by your experimental hypothesis.

5.2   RANK ORDERING OF SCORES

As we pointed out earlier, for non-parametric tests comparisons of subjects' performance are made on the basis of whether scores are higher or lower in different experimental conditions. In order to establish which scores are higher or lower it is necessary to *rank order* scores in terms of their relative size.

5.2.1   Overall Ranking of Scores

To rank scores all you have to do is assign ranks of 1, 2, 3, 4, etc. to each score in order of their magnitude, starting with the smallest, as in Table 5.

Table 5   Ranking scores

Score	Rank
6	4
3	1
12	7
4	2
7	5
5	3
8	6

You will notice that we have attributed rank 1 to the smallest score. This starting point is arbitrary. Provided that you observe the order of magnitude of the scores, there is nothing to stop you giving rank 1 to the highest score, 2 to the next highest, ending up by giving the largest rank to the smallest score. But we shall always stick to *smallest* first, as in Table 5, giving rank 1 to the smallest score of 3, rank 2 to the next smallest score of 4, and so on.

5.2.2   Zero Scores

Sometimes a subject may produce a zero score; for example, someone may not remember a single word from a text and so score 'zero' words. As far as ranks are concerned, a zero would count as the lowest possible score and so be allotted rank 1.

5.2.3   Tied Ranks

These occur when some of the scores to be ranked are the same. Look at the scores in Table 6. Three subjects produced scores of 1 and there are also two scores of 4.

Table 6   Ranking tied scores

Score	Rank
1	2
2	4
1	2
4	6.5
1	2
3	5
4	6.5
6	9
5	8

The procedure used is to give all the tied scores the *average* of the ranks they would have been entitled to. The three scores of 1 in Table 6 would have been assigned ranks 1, 2 and 3 because they are the smallest scores. So all three are given the average of these ranks, i.e.

$$\frac{1 + 2 + 3}{3} = 2$$

The next smallest score is 2. Since the ranks of 1, 2 and 3 have already been used up, this score is given rank 4. The score of 3 is given rank 5. But what about the two scores of 4? They would be entitled to the ranks of 6 and 7. Since the average of these is 6.5 they are both assigned these tied ranks. The next score of 5 can be assigned the next available rank of 8, and the biggest score of 6 gets the last rank of 9.

Question 14

Allocate ranks to the
following scores:

Score	Rank
1	
0	
2	
1	
3	

5.2.4 Ranking Differences Between Scores

So far we have been talking about overall rankings of scores in an experiment. But, as we said in Section 5.1, when we are dealing with *related designs* using the *same* (or matched) subjects, it is possible to make a direct comparison between particular subjects' scores under different experimental conditions. The easiest way to do this is to calculate the *differences* between each subject's scores for the conditions, as shown in Table 7. (Note that it is arbitrary whether you subtract Condition 1 from Condition 2 or the other way round. It is a convention, however, always to subtract Condition 2 from Condition 1 when calculating differences in scores.) Ranks are then allocated to these differences in just the same way as ranking scores.

Table 7 Ranking differences between scores

Subject	Condition 1	Condition 2	Differences (Condition 1 − Condition 2)	Ranks
1	6	5	1	2
2	7	5	2	4
3	3	2	1	2
4	5	1	4	6.5
5	5	4	1	2
6	5	2	3	5
7	5	1	4	6.5
8	4	4	0	—
9	7	1	6	9
10	6	1	5	8

5.2.5 Tied Differences Between Scores

You will notice in Table 7 that we applied exactly the same procedure for allocating tied ranks to differences as we did to scores that were the same. Thus tied ranks of 2 were given to the three differences of 1 and tied ranks of 6.5 were given to the two differences of 4.

But what about the difference of 0 produced by subject 8? Why didn't we allocate a rank to this difference just as we would have done to a zero score? The point is that subject 8 produced the same score of 4 for both Condition 1 and for Condition 2, resulting in a difference of 0. So this subject's scores do not represent a difference in favour of either experimental condition. Since this is truly a *nil* difference as far as the comparison between conditions is concerned, this kind of tie is not assigned a rank at all; in fact, it is dropped altogether from the analysis.

5.2.6 Ranking of Positive and Negative Scores

So far we have considered only positive differences between scores, but sometimes you will find negative differences as in Table 8. What you do in a case like this is to ignore the plus and minus signs completely when ranking the scores. This is because you need to know the relative magnitude of all the differences. So you count all the differences of 1 as the smallest difference, ignoring whether they are $+1$ or -1, thus ending up with a single set of ranks for all the differences.

Table 8   Ranking of positive and negative scores

Subject	Condition 1	Condition 2	Differences (Condition 1 − Condition 2)	Rank
1	3	5	− 2	
2	5	3	+ 2	
3	3	2	+ 1	
4	0	5	− 5	
5	4	4	0	
6	2	5	− 3	
7	3	5	− 2	
8	0	0	0	
9	6	1	+ 5	
10	4	5	− 1	

Question 15

On the basis of ignoring the plus and minus signs, allocate ranks to the differences in Table 8.

PROGRESS BOX SEVEN

Procedures for Rank Ordering

Overall ranking of scores (*unrelated* designs for *different* subjects)

1   Assign the lowest rank of 1 to the lowest score, the next rank of 2
    to the next lowest score, and so on.
2   *Zero scores* of 0 are counted as being the lowest possible score
    and are therefore allocated the lowest ranks.
3   When there are identical scores these are allocated *tied ranks*,
    calculated on the basis of the *average* of the ranks which should
    have been allocated to these scores.

Ranking of differences between scores (*related* designs for *same* or
matched subjects)

4   In general, ranks are assigned to *differences* between scores in
    the same way as to actual scores, with the lowest rank being allocat-
    ed to the lowest difference and so on.
5   *Tied ranks* based on average ranks are allocated to identical
    differences between scores in the same way as to identical scores.
6   *Zero scores* of 0 are counted as the lowest possible score when
    calculating differences between scores.
7   But *ties* between scores which result in a *nil* difference in favour
    of neither condition are *not* ranked and are dropped from the analy-
    sis.
8   Positive and negative differences are ranked together as a single
    series of ranks, ignoring the plus and minus signs.

5.3   NON-PARAMETRIC STATISTICAL TABLES

Each non-parametric test allows you to calculate a 'statistic' which indicates
the amount of rank-ordered differences between experimental conditions.
The statistical tables at the end of the book present, for each test, the percentage probabilities of obtaining differences in rank orders as a result of chance
fluctuations as stated by the null hypothesis. If the differences in rank-ordered
scores in your experiment are sufficiently bigger than would be expected
by chance, then these differences can be interpreted as supporting the predictions made by the experimental hypothesis ($p < .05$) or ($p < .01$).

When the results of an experiment can only be expressed in terms of
allocating subjects to *categories*, it is appropriate to use the 'statistic' known

as chi-square. This calculates the frequencies with which subjects are allocated to different categories. The chi-square statistical table provides a distribution of the percentage probabilities of obtaining different frequencies by chance. If the frequencies are unlikely to have occurred by chance ($p < .05$) or ($p < .01$), they can be considered to be significant differences as predicted by the experimental hypothesis.

If you feel uneasy about any of the terms used in this subsection, you should reread Chapter 3 in order to refresh your memory about statistical probabilities and levels of significance.

PROGRESS BOX EIGHT

1   Non-parametric tests can be used when experimental data are measured at the *ordinal* level (or in the case of chi-square at the *nominal* level).

2   With *unrelated* designs (different subjects), *all* scores are rank ordered in order to calculate overall differences between different experimental conditions. With related designs (same or matched subjects) it is the *differences* between subjects' scores under different experimental conditions which are rank ordered.

3   '*Statistics*', representing differences in rank orders between experimental conditions, can be looked up in the appropriate statistical table to find the percentage probabilities of such differences occurring by chance.

4   The chi-square 'statistic' is based on the *frequencies* with which different subjects are allocated to different categories.

CHAPTER 6

Non-Parametric Tests: Step-by-Step

We will be presenting non-parametric tests in an order which gives tests for *two* conditions first and then moves on to tests for *differences* and *trends* between *three or more* conditions. In each case, suitable tests for *related* designs are given first and then tests for *unrelated* designs, as shown in Table 9.

Table 9   Non-parametric tests

	Related designs (Same (or matched) subjects)	Unrelated designs (Different subjects)
Two conditions (ordinal data)	1 Wilcoxon	2 Mann–Whitney
Three or more conditions (ordinal data)	3 Friedman	5 Kruskal–Wallis
Trends (ordinal data)	4 Page's *L* Trend	6 Jonckheere Trend
People are allocated to two or more categories (nominal data)		7 Chi-square

The test known as chi-square comes at the end because it is different from all the other non-parametric tests. While the other tests require *ordinal* data, chi-square is only suitable for *nominal* data (see Chapter 2, Section 2.4). Instead of analysing differences between people's *scores*, it is the *people* themselves who are allocated to various categories. This distinction is discussed in full at the beginning of Section 6.7.

The detailed description for each of the tests described in this chapter is divided into five main parts.

(1) *When to use.* In this section you are reminded of the experimental designs for which you can use the test.
(2) *Example.* This gives a sample set of data which can be analysed using the test.
(3) *Rationale.* Under this heading the aims of the test are explained and information is provided to help you understand the reasons for doing the required calculations. It may be helpful to read this through rather quickly before doing the test, and then look back to it afterwards.
(4) *Step-by-step instructions.* This section provides a worked example with a clear statement of all the steps and calculations you need to carry out when doing the test.
(5) *Looking up significance in tables.* This section helps you to find your way

around statistical tables and decide whether the data in your experiment are significant.

Note about calculations

We have done all the calculations for these statistical tests with an ordinary pocket calculator. The final answers have been rounded up to a number of decimal places. If you do the calculations by hand, and/or round figures up as you go along, you may find that your answers differ from ours in the last decimal place; nothing to worry about, of course.

6.1   WILCOXON SIGNED-RANKS TEST

When to Use

The Wilcoxon test should be used for a *two condition* related design when the *same* subjects (or *matched* subjects) perform under both conditions.

Example

Suppose we want to find out whether there is a difference in the size of vocabulary used by children who go to nursery school and children who stay at home. This is a good example of a case in which a matched subjects design is essential. We obviously cannot use the same subjects since no one child can both stay at home and go to nursery school. On the other hand, we cannot just pick subjects at random for each group. For example, it may be the case that children who go to nursery school are older. Any superior effects found in this group could therefore be due to an age difference alone. The two groups of 'nursery' and 'home' children need to be matched for age, sex, intelligence and any other variables we think we may need to control. We then give the children a test which measures their vocabulary scores, as shown in Table 10.

Rationale

The aim of the Wilcoxon signed-rank tests is to compare the performance of each subject (or pairs of subjects) to find out whether there are significant differences between their scores under the two conditions. The scores of Condition B are subtracted from those of Condition A, and the resulting differences (d) are given a plus (+) or, if negative, a minus (−) sign. These differences are ranked in order of magnitude (irrespective of plus or minus signs). The ranks are then added up separately for the plus signs and the

Table 10   Vocabulary scores of children who go to nursery school or stay at home

Subject pair	Condition A (vocabulary scores of children at home)	Condition B (vocabulary scores of children at nursery)	d (A − B)	Rank of d	Rank of plus differences	Rank of minus differences
1	3	5	− 2	5(−)		5
2	4	5	− 1	2(−)		2
3	3	2	+ 1	2(+)	2	
4	1	5	− 4	8.5(−)		8.5
5	5	4	+ 1	2(+)	2	
6	2	5	− 3	7(−)		7
7	3	5	− 2	5(−)		5
8	4	4	0	Omit tie		
9	1	5	− 4	8.5(−)		8.5
10	3	5	− 2	5(−)		5
Total	29	45			4	41
Mean	2.9	4.5				

minus signs. The smaller of these rank totals gives the value of a statistic called W which can be looked up in the appropriate table for significance.

The idea is that if there are only chance differences, as stated by the null hypothesis, then there should be roughly equal numbers of high and low ranks for the plus and minus differences. If there is a preponderance of *low* ranks for one sign, this means that there must be a lot of high ranks for the other sign, indicating larger differences in favour of one condition than would be expected by chance. Because the statistic W reflects the smaller total of ranks, the *smaller W is, the more significant* are the differences in ranks between the two conditions.

Step-by-Step Instructions for Calculating the Value of W

1	Calculate the difference d between each pair of scores, assigning plus or minus signs	See column $d(A − B)$ in Table 10
2	Rank the differences in order of magnitude from the smallest (rank) to the largest *ignoring* plus and minus signs (see Chapter 5, Section 5.2 for instructions about how to rank scores)	See column *Rank of d* in Table 10

3 Add together separately the ranks corresponding to the different signs	See totals for *Rank of plus differences* and *Rank of minus differences* columns in Table 10
4 Take the smaller of the rank totals as W	Observed value of $W = 4$ (since the rank total for the plus differences is the smaller)
5 Count the number of pairs of subjects N (not counting ties)	$N = 10 - 1 = 9$

Looking up Significance of W in Table A

Table A gives the level of significance of W for both a one-tailed test and a two-tailed test. In the left-hand column are the values of N. Since we did *not* make a prediction in one particular direction, e.g. that there would be higher vocabulary scores for nursery school children, we have to use the levels of significance for a two-tailed hypothesis. Select the appropriate value $N = 9$ and look along that row to see whether your observed value of W is significant. Since the convention is to take the *smaller* total of ranks, the observed value of W will have to be *equal* to or *smaller* than the critical values in the table. As the observed value of $W = 4$ is *less* than the critical value of 6 for $p < .05$ (two-tailed), you can reject the null hypothesis and conclude that there is a *significant* difference between the vocabulary scores for the two groups of matched subjects.

Suppose you had made a one-tailed prediction in one direction, say, that children who go to nursery school (Condition B) will score higher on the vocabulary test. The observed W value of 4 is smaller than 6, the critical value of W for $p < .025$ (one-tailed), a lower probability, and therefore more significant, than the two tailed $p < .05$ significance level, as you would expect (see Chapter 4, Section 4.3.2). Naturally you will have to check in Table 10 that the results of your experiment are in the predicted direction, i.e. that the mean vocabulary scores for the nursery school children *are* higher than those for the home children.

Remember that all of the above step-by-step instructions apply to experiments in which the *same* (rather than matched) subjects perform under both conditions.

Question 16

To test the effects of sentence length on comprehension, twelve subjects were each asked to read two texts matched for content difficulty. In one of the texts ideas were expressed in short, precise sentences; in the other, ideas were expressed in long, complex sentences. The experimental hypothesis predicted that short sentence texts would be easier to understand. (See Table over page.)

Comprehension scores were as follows:

Subject	Condition 1 (short sentences)	Condition 2 (long sentences)
1	15	10
2	12	14
3	11	11
4	16	11
5	14	4
6	13	1
7	11	12
8	8	10

(a) Calculate the mean scores for the two conditions.
(b) Is there a significant difference in the predicted direction? Look back to the step-by-step instructions for calculating the value of W.

6.2 MANN–WHITNEY TEST

When to Use

The Mann–Whitney test should be used for a *two condition* unrelated design when *different* subject are used for each of the conditions.

Example

Suppose we want to find out the effect of meaningful material on memory recall. One group of six subjects are asked to learn not very meaningful material and another group of six subjects are asked to learn meaningful material (Table 11). Memory is measured by the number of words recalled and we predict that recall scores will be higher for Condition 2.

Rationale

The rationale behind the Mann–Whitney test is very similar to that of the Wilcoxon test. The basic difference between the two is due to the difference between a related design using the same subjects and an unrelated design using different subjects. The Wilcoxon analyses the differences between the performance of the *same* subjects (or matched pairs of subjects) under two experimental conditions. With an unrelated design there is no basis for

Table 11   Recall scores for meaningful and less meaningful material

Condition 1 (unmeaningful material) scores	Rank (1)	Condition 2 (meaningful material) scores	Rank (2)
3	3	9	11
4	4	7	9
2	1.5	5	5.5
6	7.5	10	12
2	1.5	6	7.5
5	5.5	8	10
Total 22	$T_1 = 23$	45	$T_2 = 55$
Mean 3.67		7.5	

comparing differences between pairs of scores. So the Mann–Whitney test ranks the scores of all the different subjects in both conditions as if they were a single set of scores.

If the differences between conditions are chance differences, as stated by the null hypothesis, then there should be roughly equal scores and, therefore, roughly equal ranks in the two conditions. If there is a preponderance of low or high ranks in one condition or the other, then the difference in the total of ranked scores for each condition is likely to be due not to chance but to the predicted effects of the independent variable. If the total of ranks for one of the conditions is very small then there must be a preponderance of high ranks in the other condition. A statistic called U reflects the smaller total of ranks. The *smaller U is*, the more significant the differences in ranks between the two conditions.

Step-by-step Instructions for Calculating the Value of U

1   Rank all the scores for both groups as a single series of ranks, giving 1 to lowest score and so on (see Chapter 5, Section 5.2, for instructions about how to rank scores)

   Overall ranking of all scores is shown in *Rank* (1) and *Rank* (2) columns taken together in Table 11

2   Add the rank totals for Group 1 and Group 2 separately

   $T_1 = 23, T_2 = 55$

3   Select the larger total of ranks

   $T_2 = 55$

4   Find the value of U from the formula

$$U = n_1 n_2 + \frac{n_x(n_x + 1)}{2} - T_x$$

where

n_1 = number of subjects in $n_1 = 6$
    Group 1

n_2 = number of subjects in $n_1 = 6$
    Group 2

T_x = largest rank total $T_x = T_2 = 55$

n_x = number of subjects in the $n_x = n_2 = 6$
    group with the largest rank
    total

Calculate $U = 6 \times 6 + \dfrac{6 \times 7}{2} - 55$

$$= 36 + 21 - 55$$
$$= 2$$

Note that when there are *equal* numbers of subjects in each condition it is easy to see which is the largest rank total. Generally, it is preferable to have equal numbers of subjects in each group. However, if there do turn out to be *unequal* numbers of subjects in each group, you would have to allow for this. If in doubt, calculate U for both rank totals, selecting the appropriate n_x in each case, and then take the *smaller U*. As we expect you can see, the whole point of having n_x in the formula for U is to allow for the case when there *are* unequal numbers of subjects in the two groups, i.e. when n_1 and n_2 are *not* the same.

Looking up Significance in Tables B(1)–(4)

Tables B(1)–(4) give you the critical values of U at different levels of significance for one-tailed and two-tailed tests for different combinations of n_1 and n_2 for the two groups. You have to locate the appropriate table from B(1)–(4).

The usual procedure is to start with Tables B(3) or B(4) to see if the value of U is significant at the $p < .05$ level for a one-tailed test (B(4)) or for a two-tailed test (B(3)). Since we predicted that the Condition 2 subjects who were learning meaningful material would have higher recall scores, we can look at Table B(4). Locate $n_1 = 6$ along the top and $n_2 = 6$ down the side and at the intersection you will find the critical value of U. Since it is a convention to use the smaller value of U, our observed value of $U = 2$ must be *equal* to or *less* than the critical value of 7, which it is. Moving to Table B(3) our observed U value of 2 is smaller than the critical value of 5 for $n_1 = 6$ and $n_2 = 6$. In Table B(2) our observed U value of 2 is less than the critical value of 3. In Table B(1) our observed U value of 2 is equal to the critical value at $n_1 = 6$ and $n_2 = 6$. We can therefore reject the null hypothesis and accept that there is a significant difference in favour of remembering meaningful material ($p < .005$); checking, of course, in Table 11 that the difference between the means *is* in that direction.

If we had made a two-tailed prediction that there would be an effect in either direction, then the significance level from Table B(1) would have been only $p < .01$ (i.e. a 1 in 100 probability of a chance result rather than 5 in 1000).

Question 17

Twenty six-letter words were presented at a fast rate on a screen to two groups of different subjects. For Group 1 the words were presented on the left-hand side of the screen. For Group 2 the words were presented on the right-hand side of the screen. The number of words recognized were as follows: Group 1 (left-hand side presentation) 18, 15, 17, 13, 11, 16, 10, 17; Group 2 (right-hand side presentation) 17, 13, 12, 16, 10, 15, 11, 13, 12. The experimental hypothesis stated that subjects given the words on the left-hand side of the screen would perform better due to the effects of left to right reading in our culture.

Note that there are eight subjects in Group 1 and nine subjects in Group 2. This will affect both the calculation of U, since you will have to use a different n_x for the two groups, and the n_1 and n_2 for looking up significance in Tables B(1)–(4).

(a) Is the experimental hypothesis one- or two-tailed?
(b) What are the mean scores for each group?
(c) Can the experimental hypothesis be accepted at the $p < .05$ level of significance?

6.3 FRIEDMAN TEST

When to Use

This test can be considered as an extension of the Wilcoxon test when it is necessary to use *three or more* conditions. It should be used for a *related* design when the *same* subjects (or *matched* subjects) are performing under *three or more* conditions.

Example

Suppose a publisher producing a series of children's books wants to choose from three types of illustrations the one which is most appealing to children. Eight children are asked to rate all three illustrations on a five point scale from 1 'not good at all' to 5 'extremely good', producing rating scores as shown in Table 12.

Table 12   Ratings of three kinds of illustrations

Subject	Condition 1 (illustration A)		Condition 2 (illustration B)		Condition 3 (illustration C)	
	Rating Score	Rank	Rating Score	Rank	Rating Score	Rank
1	2	1	5	3	4	2
2	1	1	5	3	3	2
3	3	1	5	2.5	5	2.5
4	3	2	5	3	2	1
5	2	1	3	2	5	3
6	1	1	4	2.5	4	2.5
7	5	3	3	2	2	1
8	1	1	4	3	3	2
Total	18	11	34	21	28	16
Mean	2.25		4.25		3.50	

Rationale

Since this is a related design in which each subject produces scores for all conditions, it is permissible to compare scores for each subject *across* conditions to see under which conditions they produce small or large scores. Because there are more than two conditions, it is not possible to calculate differences between the scores for two conditions as was the case with the Wilcoxon test. Instead we rank order the scores for each subject *horizontally* across the rows for the three conditions as shown in Table 12. For example, subject 1's scores of 2 for Condition 1, 5 for Condition 2 and 4 for Condition 3 are allocated three ranks from smallest to largest: rank 1 for Condition 1, rank 2 for Condition 3 and rank 3 for Condition 2; and similarly for the other subjects. Of course, if there were *four* experimental conditions we would rank the scores for each subject from 1 to 4.

The next step is to add up the totals of ranks for each condition. If there are only chance differences between the scores under all conditions, as stated by the null hypothesis, we would expect these rank totals to be approximately equal, since there would be some low ranks (low scores) and some high ranks (high scores) in each of the conditions. However, if the conditions are significantly different, we would expect to get quite different rank totals, with some conditions having a preponderance of low ranks and some a preponderance of high ranks. The size of the differences between rank totals is given by a statistic called Xr^2. If the observed value of Xr^2 is *equal* to or *larger* than the critical values in Tables C and D, the implication is that the differences in the rank totals for the different conditions are large enough to be significant.

Step-by-Step Instructions for Calculating the Value of Xr^2

1   Rank the scores for each separate subject *across* each row, giving 1 to the smallest score and so on (see Chapter 5, Section 5.2 for instructions about how to rank scores)

See *Rank* columns in Table 12. Note that the ranks for each row of scores are equivalent to ranks 1, 2, 3, since there are three conditions (sometimes tied, e.g. 2.5)

2   Add the total of ranks for each condition

Rank totals in Table 12 are 11, 21, 16

3   Find the value of Xr^2 from the formula:

$$Xr^2 = \left[\frac{12}{N C(C+1)} \sum T_c^2 \right] - 3N(C+1)$$

where

C = number of conditions $C = 3$
N = number of subjects (or sets $N = 8$
of matched subjects)

T_c = total of ranks for each condition $T_1 = 11, T_2 = 21, T_3 = 16$

T_c^2 = squares of the rank total for $T_1^2 = 11^2, T_2^2 = 21^2, T_3^2 = 16^2$
each condition

$\sum$ means *sum* (i.e. add up) any symbols which follow it

$\sum T_c^2$ = sum of the squared rank $11^2 + 21^2 + 16^2$
totals for each condition

Calculate $Xr^2 = \left[\left(\frac{12}{(8 \times 3)(3+1)} \right)(11^2 + 21^2 + 16^2) \right] - 3 \times 8(3+1)$

$= \left[\left(\frac{12}{24 \times 4} \right)(121 + 441 + 256) \right] - (24 \times 4)$

$= \left(\frac{12}{96} \times 818 \right) - 96$

$= 102.25 - 96$

$= 6.25$

4   Calculate the degrees of freedom $df = C - 1 = 3 - 1 = 2$
    i.e. number of conditions (C)
    minus one (see Chapter 4, Section
    4.3.1)

Looking up Significance of Xr^2 in Tables C and D

There are two tables to look up the critical values of Xr^2. One of them, Table C, is used when the numbers of conditions and subjects are small. Table C(1) gives Xr^2 values for three conditions when N (number of subjects) equals anything from 2 to 9. Table C(2) gives Xr^2 values for four conditions when N (number of subjects) equals 2, 3 or 4. Table D is the chi-square distribution table. You can refer to it when your sample of subjects is larger than those in Tables C(1) and C(2) because Xr^2 has a similar distribution to chi-square.

The table you should consult to look up the observed value of Xr^2 for this experiment is Table C(1) because *eight* subjects are performing under *three* conditions. All you have to do is to locate the appropriate column for N (number of subjects or sets of matched subjects) and find in the p column the nearest probability which is less than one of the conventional levels of significance. Looking at the probabilities for $N = 8$, the observed value of $Xr^2 = 6.25$ is equivalent to a probability of $p < .047$. We hope you can see that this probability is less than $p < .05$, one of the conventional levels of significance. To achieve the $p < .01$ level of significance our value of Xr^2 would have had to be 9.00 since $p < .009$ is less than $p < .01$. If your Xr^2 value is not given in the table, you should take the next smallest value when looking up probabilities. For instance, if our value of Xr^2 had been 5.95 we would have had to take the probability given for 5.25, i.e. $p < .079$, which is greater than $p < .05$ and therefore not significant. To look up values in Table C(2) you should follow the same procedure as for Table C(1).

If you did have more conditions and/or subjects and had to consult Table D, all you have to do is locate the value of the degrees of freedom down the left-hand column (in our example $df = 2$, i.e. number of conditions $- 1$). Then look along the row of probabilities until you find one of the conventional levels of significance. Our observed value of $Xr^2 = 6.25$ is larger than the critical value of 5.99 shown in the chi-square table, so we can accept that our results are significant at the $p < .05$ level of significance. However, since our observed value of Xr^2 is less than the critical value of 9.21 for $p < .01$, we cannot reject the null hypothesis at this level of significance.

From the statistical analysis of the experiment you can conclude that the children showed significantly different preferences for the three types of illustration. It appears from the means in Table 12 that they preferred illustration B, since this received the highest ratings, with illustration C next and illustration A last. However the Friedman test can only tell you that there are overall differences between the conditions. To see if there is a *trend* in favour of the illustrations in a particular order you need to use a trend test. For related designs the appropriate trend test is Page's *L* trend test which is described in Section 6.4.

Question 18

Five subjects were given three different passages of prose to read. Scores were the number of ideas recalled by subjects in their accounts of the passages. In Condition 1, scores were 4, 2, 6, 3, 3; in Condition 2: 5, 7, 6, 7, 8, and in Condition 3: 6, 7, 8, 5, 9.
(a) What are the mean scores for each of the three conditions?
(b) Are the differences between the scores of the three conditions significant? If so, at what level of significance?

6.4   PAGE'S *L* TREND TEST

When to Use

This test can be thought of as an extension of the Friedman test when you need to look at *trends* between *three or more conditions*. It should be used for a *related* design when *same* (or *matched*) subjects are doing all conditions.

Example

We shall use the same example as that for the Friedman test. From the results of such an experiment we might wish to predict that there is a significant *trend* in the children's ratings for each illustration in the order of greatest preference for illustration B, followed by illustrations C and A. In order to test this we *rearrange* the order of conditions in the predicted order. This means that the original order of Conditions 1, 2, 3 in Table 12 becomes 1, 3, 2, indicating an order from lowest to highest rating scores, as shown in Table 13.

Rationale

The rationale behind the test is exactly the same as that for the Friedman test, except that this time we are predicting that the rank totals will fall in a certain order, from the *smallest* on the left to the *largest* on the right-hand side of the table. It is important to remember that the conditions

Table 13 Ratings of three kinds of illustrations in the predicted order

Subject	Condition 1 (same) (illustration A) Rating Score	Rank	Condition 2 (old 3) (illustration C) Rating Score	Rank	Condition 3 (old 2) (illustration B) Rating Scores	Rank
1	2	1	4	2	5	3
2	1	1	3	2	5	3
3	3	1	5	2.5	5	2.5
4	3	2	2	1	5	3
5	2	1	5	3	3	2
6	1	1	4	2.5	4	2.5
7	5	3	2	1	3	2
8	1	1	3	2	4	3
Total	18	11	28	16	34	21
Mean	2.25		3.50		4.25	

should appear in the table of results in the predicted order from the group whose scores are predicted to be the lowest on the left to the group whose scores are predicted to be the largest on the right.

As with the Friedman test you should start by ranking the three conditions for each subject *separately across* conditions. The next step is to add up the ranks for each condition. If there are no significant differences between the conditions, as stated by the null hypothesis, we would expect these rank totals to be approximately equal, since there would be some high ranks and some low ranks in each of the conditions. However, if there is a significant trend in scores, we would expect the rank totals to occur in the predicted order from the smallest on the left to the highest on the right.

The trend in rank total differences is given by a statistic called L. Since L reflects the size of the differences between rank totals in the predicted direction, the value of L should be *equal* to or *larger* than the critical values in Table E.

Step-by-Step Instructions for Calculating the Value of L

1	Rank the scores for each subject across each row *separately* (as with the Friedman test)	See *Rank* columns in Table 13, allocating ranks 1, 2, 3, across the three conditions *for each subject separately*

2   Add the ranks for each condition   Rank totals in Table 13 are 11, 16, 21

3   Find the value of L from the formula

$$L = \sum(T_c \times c)$$

where

T_c = total of ranks for each condition $T_1 = 11, T_2 = 16, T_3 = 21$

c = numbers allotted to the Conditions 1, 2, 3 from left to right

$(T_c \times c)$ = the rank total for each $T_1 \times 1 = 11 \times 1$

condition multiplied by its $T_2 \times 2 = 16 \times 2$

respective condition number $T_3 \times 3 = 21 \times 3$

$\sum$ means to *sum* (i.e. add up) any symbols which follow it

Calculate $L = (11 \times 1) + (16 \times 2) + (21 \times 3)$

$= 11 + 32 + 63$

$= 106$

4   Find number of conditions (C) $C = 3,$
and number of subjects (N) $N = 8$

Looking up Significance of L in Table E

The critical value of L is dependent upon the number of subjects (or sets of matched subjects) and the number of conditions (up to 6). When you refer to Table E locate the number of conditions (C) used in your experiment (in our example 3) along the top row of the table, and the number of subjects (N) (in our example 8) down the left- hand column. At the intersection of the N row and the C column you will find the critical value of L for three levels of significance. The upper figure in each group gives the value of L for $p < .001$, the middle figure gives L for $p < .01$ and the lower figure gives L for $p < .05$ (see final column in Table E). The observed value of L has to be *equal* to or *larger* than the critical value to reach significance. In our example, the observed value of $L = 106$ is equal to the critical value for the $p < .01$ level of significance, so you can reject the null hypothesis and conclude that there is a significant trend in the children's rating preferences in the predicted order $(p < .01)$. Note that the distribution of L in Table E only applies to a one-tailed hypothesis, when a trend is predicted in one particular direction.

Question 19

Five subjects were given three texts to read and were told that they would be asked for verbatim recall. In Condition 1 the sentences were short; in Condition 2 the sentences were of medium length and in Condition 3 the sentences were long. The experimenter predicted that the number of correct sentences recalled would decrease across the three conditions, i.e. most sentences recalled in Condition 1, significantly less in Conditions 2 and 3. Results were as follows: Condition 1: 8, 10, 9, 7, 11; Condition 2: 7, 5, 2, 4, 5; Condition 3: 3, 3, 4, 1, 6.

(a) Looking at the mean scores for the conditions, is there likely to be a trend in the predicted direction?
(b) Can the null hypothesis be rejected at the $p < .001$ level of significant?
(c) Are the results significant at any level of significance?

6.5   KRUSKAL–WALLIS TEST

When to Use

This test can be considered as an extension of the Mann–Whitney test when we need to use *three or more* conditions. It should be used for an *unrelated* design when *different* subjects are performing under *three or more* conditions.

Example

Suppose we are interested in finding out whether there are significant differences in the learning of three types of texts: highly illustrated, some illustrations and no illustrations. We allocate *different* subjects to each of the three experimental conditions and assess their performance by the number of ideas they recall, as shown in Table 14.

Table 14   Number of ideas recalled for three types of text

	Group 1 subjects (highly illustrated text)		Group 2 subjects (text with some illustrations)		Group 3 subjects (text with no illustrations)	
	Score	Rank	Score	Rank	Score	Rank
	19	10	14	6	12	3.5
	21	11	15	7	12	3.5
	17	9	9	1	13	5
	16	8			10	2
Total	73	38	38	14	47	14
Mean	18.25		12.67		11.75	

Rationale

The aim of the test is to determine whether scores for three or more groups of subjects are significantly different. Because the scores all come from *different* subjects the only way to look at differences between conditions is to rank all the scores together in a single series, as with the Mann–Whitney test. (This is because, since all the subjects are different, there is no basis for comparing scores of the same subjects or matched subjects across conditions as with the Friedman test for related designs.) These overall ranks are added up for each column separately to produce a total of ranks for each condition. If there are only chance differences between the conditions, as stated by the null hypothesis, we would expect high and low ranks to be spread roughly equally among the conditions. But, if there is a preponderance of high or low ranks in one or other of the different conditions, it is more likely that these reflect significant differences due to the independent variable.

The value of the differences between rank totals is given by a statistic called H. Since the experimental hypothesis predicts that there will be large differences between conditions, the observed value of H should be *equal* to or *larger* than the critical values in Table F in order to be significant.

Step-by-Step Instructions for Calculating the Value of H

1 Rank all the scores for all the groups as a single series of ranks giving 1 to the smallest score and so on (see Chapter 5, Section 5.2)

See *Rank* columns for Groups 1, 2 and 3 in Table 14 for overall ranking of all scores taken together

2 Add the totals of ranks for each condition

Rank totals in Table 14 are 38, 14, 14

3 Find the value of H from the following formula:

$$H = \left[\frac{12}{N(N+1)} \sum \frac{T_c^2}{n_c} \right] - 3(N+1)$$

where

N = total number of subjects

$N = 11$

n_c = number of subjects in each group

$n_1 = 4, n_2 = 3, n_3 = 4$

T_c = totals of ranks for each condition, i.e. the rank totals for each column

$T_1 = 38, T_2 = 14, T_3 = 14$

T_c^2 = squares of the rank total for each condition

$T_1^2 = 38^2, T_2^2 = 14^2, T_3^2 = 14^2$

$\sum$ means to *sum* (i.e. add up) any symbols which follow it

$\dfrac{\sum T_c^2}{n_c}$ = the sum of the squared rank totals for each condition divided by the number of subjects in that condition

$\sum \dfrac{T_c^2}{n_c} = \dfrac{38^2}{4} + \dfrac{14^2}{3} + \dfrac{14^2}{4}$

Calculate
$$H = \left[\frac{12}{11 \times 12} \left(\frac{38^2}{4} + \frac{14^2}{3} + \frac{14^2}{4} \right) \right] - 3 \times 12$$

$$= \left[\frac{12}{132} \left(\frac{1444}{4} + \frac{196}{3} + \frac{196}{4} \right) \right] - 36$$

$$= .091(361 + 65.33 + 49) - 36$$

$$= 43.255 - 36$$

$$= 7.26$$

4 Calculate the degrees of freedom, i.e. number of conditions (C) minus one

$df = C - 1 = 3 - 1 = 2$

Looking up Significance in Tables F and D

Table F covers experiments for *three* groups of subjects with up to five subjects in each group. For more subjects Table D—the chi-square table— should be used. In the left-hand column of Table F you will see the numbers of subjects for each group when no more than three groups are being tested. Locate the relevant combination (in our example 4, 4, 3). Note that the *order* of the numbers of subjects for each group does not matter. In our experiment the group sizes were $n_1 = 4$, $n_2 = 3$ and $n_3 = 4$. But the appropriate combination in Table F is 4, 4, 3. Against this you will find critical values of H for various probabilities. If the observed value of H is *equal* to or *larger* than the critical value for a particular level of significance, you can reject the null hypothesis. In our example, our observed value of $H = 7.26$ is larger than the critical value of 7.1439 for $p < .01$, so we can accept the experimental hypothesis at this level of significance.

If you have more than three conditions, and/or more subjects in each condition, you must find the critical value in Table D, the chi-square table. Note that for this you need the calculated degrees of freedom. Locate the value of the degrees of freedom (in our example $df = 2$) down the left-hand column and look along the row of critical values for the different probabilities. Our observed value of $H = 7.26$ is larger than the critical value of 5.99 for $p < .05$, so we can accept that the result is significant at this level. You will notice that this probability is less significant than when we used Table F. This is because Table F is especially designed to give the probabilities for small numbers of conditions and subjects. You should also note that the Kruskal–Wallis test can only tell you that there are overall differences in recall scores between experimental conditions. In Table 14 it looks as if there is a trend in the means from the most illustrated text down to the text with no illustrations. But to test this you will need to use the Jonckheere trend test for unrelated designs given in Section 6.6.

Question 20

An experimenter wanted to investigate the effect that different types of instruction have on solving problems. One group of subjects was given written instructions. A second group of subjects was shown how the puzzle was solved but had no written instructions. The third group of subjects was given written instructions *and* shown how to proceed according to them. The three groups were then asked to solve the puzzle. Scores were obtained by counting the number of wrong moves made. Scores for Group 1 were: 20, 27, 19, 23; Group 2: 25, 33, 35, 36; Group 3: 19, 20, 25, 22.

(a) What are the mean scores for each group?
(b) Is the observed value of H significant?

6.6 JONCKHEERE TREND TEST

When to Use

The Jonckheere trend test can be thought of as an extension of the Kruskal–Wallis test for looking at *trends* between *three or more* experimental conditions. It should be used for an *unrelated* design when *different* subjects perform under different experimental conditions.

Example

We shall use the example worked out for the Kruskal–Wallis test when we tested the learning of three different types of illustrated texts, allocating different subjects to each text. Suppose that this time we predict that subjects' scores will show a trend so that they recall a significantly greater number of ideas from the highly illustrated texts, fewer ideas from the text with some illustrations and least ideas from the non-illustrated text. Because we are predicting a trend in that direction, we have to *rearrange* the experimental conditions from left to right to give the order of no illustrations (which is predicted to produce the *lowest* scores), some illustrations next and finally highly illustrated (which should produce the *highest* scores). Notice that this is *opposite* to the way we had the conditions in Table 14. It is a general convention with trend tests to order the conditions in the predicted order from lowest scores on the left to highest scores on the right.

As is often the case, it is advisable to have *equal* numbers of subjects under each condition, and for the Jonckheere test it is essential. We have therefore assumed that four subjects were tested in each of the three conditions, so that Group 2 has an extra subject in Table 15, as compared with Table 14.

Table 15 Number of ideas recalled for three types of texts

	Conditions		
	Group 1 subjects (text with no illustrations)	Group 2 subjects (text with some illustrations)	Group 3 subjects (highly illustrated text)
	12 (7)	14 (4)	19
	12 (7)	15 (4)	21
	13 (6)	9 (4)	17
	10 (7)	13 (4)	16
Mean	11.75	12.75	18.25

Rationale

The rationale behind the Jonckheere trend test is different from those so far described. Instead of ranking the scores first, what the test does is to count the number of scores which are higher in each condition than scores in previous conditions. If there are only chance differences, as stated by the null hypothesis, the scores in each condition should be roughly equal and there should be no reason for the scores in any of the conditions to be higher than in the others. But, if there is a preponderance of scores that are higher in the right-hand columns, then this means that there is a trend from lowest scores on the left to highest scores on the right, as predicted by the experimental hypothesis. Any preponderance of higher scores in the right-hand conditions is given by a statistic called S. Since the prediction is that there will be a significant trend from left to right, the observed value of S should be *equal* to or *larger* than the critical values in Table G to be significant.

Step-by-Step Instructions for Calculating S

1   Starting with the left-hand group, for *each* separate score count up the number of scores in all the conditions to the *right* of Group 1 which are higher than that score. For example, for the first score of 12 in Group 1 the following scores in Group 2 are higher, 14, 15 (*not* 9), 13 and in Group 3, 19, 21, 17, 16 which adds up to (7) higher scores. Do the same for the scores in Group 2

Do *not* include ties *across* conditions when calculating the numbers of higher scores, e.g. when doing the third score of 13 in Group 1, only the 14 and the 15 in Group 2 are counted as being higher (*not* the tied 13), which together with the four higher scores in Group 3 makes the total for that score (6)

The numbers in brackets in Table 15 represent the numbers of higher scores for each score. All the scores in Group 2 obtain values of (4) since, for each score, the four scores in Group 3 are higher. Note that there are no brackets against Group 3, since there are obviously *no* scores to the *right* of this condition

2   Add up the sum of the figures in brackets. Call this sum A

$A = 7 + 7 + 6 + 7 + 4 + 4 + 4 + 4$
$\quad = 43$

3   Find the maximum value that A
     could have (i.e. if *all* the scores in
     the right-hand columns were
     higher than all the scores in the
     left-hand columns) from the for-
     mula

$$B = \frac{C(C - 1)}{2} \times n^2$$

where
C = number of conditions $C = 3$
n = number of subjects in each $n = 4$
     condition

Calculate $B = \dfrac{3(3 - 1)}{2} \times 4^2$

$$= \frac{3 \times 2}{2} \times 16$$

$$= 3 \times 16$$

$$= 48$$

4   Calculate the value of S by $S = (2 \times 43) - 48$
     substituting A and B in the $= 86 - 48$
     following formula $= 38$

$$S = 2A - B$$

Looking up Significance in Table G

Table G gives you critical values of S depending on the number of subjects
in each condition (n up to 10) and number of conditions (C up to 6) for two
levels of significance ($p < .05$ and $p < .01$). If the observed value of S is
equal to or *larger* than the critical value for a particular level of significance,
you can reject the null hypothesis. For $n = 4$ and $C = 3$ our observed value
of $S = 38$ is *larger* than the critical value of 24 for $p < .05$. We now look at
the critical value for $p < .01$ and find that our observed S value of 38 is
greater than the critical value of 32 for this level of significance too. So we
can reject the null hypothesis at a $p < .01$ level of significance and conclude
that there is a significant trend in recall scores from most ideas remembered for highly illustrated down to least ideas for texts with no illustrations,
as indicated by the mean scores in Table 15.

Question 21

Turn back to Question 20. Suppose the experimenter had predicted that subjects in Group 3 would perform significantly better than subjects in Group 1 and that these would in turn perform significantly better than subjects in Group 2.

(a) Is the predicted trend significant at the $p < .01$ level?
(b) Is it significant at the $p < .05$ level?

6.7   CHI–SQUARE TEST

When to Use

The chi-square test is the only suitable test to use when the data from your experiment is *nominal* (see Chapter 2, Section 2.4). This means that instead of being able to measure your subjects' scores you can only allocate *subjects* to one or more *categories*. Because subjects cannot be allocated to more than one category, the chi-square test is only appropriate for making predictions about how many *different* subjects will fall into each category.

One point must be taken into consideration when using the chi-square. In all the other experimental designs discussed so far, the experimenter decides how many subjects to have in each group and so the number of scores in each group is predetermined. However, the chi-square tests an experimental hypothesis which predicts how many subjects in each group will fall into certain categories; so this cannot be decided in advance. Consequently, you have to test quite a lot of subjects to make sure that a sufficient number of subjects turn out to be allocated to each category. The minimum is usually considered to be at least twenty subjects. This may sound rather a lot, but it does not usually take too long to carry out an experiment in which you are only going to allocate subjects to categories.

Example

Suppose we want to find out whether social science students employ a method of study which is significantly different from that used by technology students. We choose two groups, one group of 50 social science students and one group of 50 technology students. We send out a questionnaire to all 100 students asking them to indicate whether their study method falls into one of three study patterns: regular day-to-day study, irregular concentrated bursts of intensive work or a mixture of both. We receive 44 replies from social science students and 42 replies from technology students. We then allocate these replies into one or other of our three categories, regular, irregular or mixed study. The results are shown in the form of a 2 × 3 table known as a contingency table. The 'cells' representing each of the categories are numbered 1 to 6 in Table 16. Remember that the figures in the table represent the number of *subjects* who fall into each category; they are *not* scores obtained from subjects (as was the case in all the previous tests described in this book).

Table 16   Contingency table (2 rows × 3 columns)

	Regular	Study patterns Irregular	Mixed	Marginal totals of students
Group 1 Social science students	1 6 $E = 8.19$	2 15 $E = 11.77$	3 23 $E = 24.05$	44
Group 2 Technology students	4 10 $E = 7.81$	5 8 $E = 11.23$	6 24 $E = 22.95$	42
Marginal totals of study patterns	16	23	47	Grand total (N) 86

Rationale

What the chi-square test does is to compare the *observed* frequencies in each of the squares (cells) of a contingency table with the *expected* frequencies (E) for each cell if the differences are due to chance, as stated by the null hypothesis. In other words, the test compares the actual numbers of students who fall into each cell as against the numbers of students we would expect to fall into each cell if there were in fact no differences between the study patterns of the two types of students. We already know the *observed* frequencies resulting from our experiment (as shown in Table 16). But we have to estimate the *expected* chance frequencies from the numbers of each type of student and the distribution of study patterns, which are given in the marginal totals in Table 16. We know that, overall, there are 44 social science students and 42 technology students. But, in order to calculate the expected frequencies, we also have to consider the number of students who use each of the study patterns. For instance, we have to take into account the fact that only 16 students out of a total of 86 showed regular study patterns when calculating our expected frequencies for that study pattern. Thus, we can work out the proportions of the 44 social science students and the 42 technology students who would be expected to have this study pattern if there were no real differences between the types of students. Similarly, expected frequencies can be calculated for the other cells on the basis of the overall number of students with irregular (23) and mixed (47) study patterns.

If the observed results are due to chance they should approximate closely to these expected frequencies. But, if the observed frequencies in the cells differ significantly from the expected frequencies, then the experimental hypothesis is supported. The statistic χ^2 (pronounced chi-square) reflects the size of the differences between observed and expected frequencies. The *greater* the difference between observed and expected frequencies the more likely the result is to be significant; so the computed value of χ^2 should be *equal* to or *larger* than the critical values given in Table D.

On the question of appropriate number of subjects, the calculated *expected* frequencies should ideally come out to a minimum of 5 for each cell. This applies particularly when you only have two groups allocated to two categories, giving only four cells. When you have six cells, as in the 2 × 3 table shown in Table 16, you can still use the test if the number of expected frequencies in just one of the cells is under 5. Note that this requirement applies only to the expected frequencies. It does not matter how many of the *observed* frequencies are less than 5, i.e. the numbers of actual subjects who fall into each category.

Step-by-Step Instructions for Calculating the Value of χ^2

1 Calculate the expected frequencies (E) for each cell by multiplying the two relevant marginal totals for each cell and dividing by the total number of subjects N.

$$\text{Cell 1: } E = \frac{16 \times 44}{86} = 8.19$$

$$\text{Cell 2: } E = \frac{23 \times 44}{86} = 11.77$$

$$\text{Cell 3: } E = \frac{47 \times 44}{86} = 24.05$$

Cells are numbered 1 to 6 in Table 16 (marginal totals of study patterns are given first)

$$\text{Cell 4: } E = \frac{16 \times 42}{86} = 7.81$$

$$\text{Cell 5: } E = \frac{23 \times 42}{86} = 11.23$$

$$\text{Cell 6: } E = \frac{47 \times 42}{86} = 22.95$$

2   Find the value of χ^2 from the formula:

$$\chi^2 = \sum \frac{(O - E)^2}{E}$$

where

   O = observed frequencies for each cell (as shown in Table 16)

   E = expected frequencies for each cell (as calculated above)

   $\sum$ = add up the results of $\frac{(O - E)^2}{E}$ calculated for each cell

$$\chi^2 = \frac{(6 - 8.19)^2}{8.19}$$

$$+ \frac{(15 - 11.77)^2}{11.77}$$

$$+ \frac{(23 - 24.05)^2}{24.05}$$

$$+ \frac{(10 - 7.81)^2}{7.81}$$

$$+ \frac{(8 - 11.23)^2}{11.23}$$

$$+ \frac{(24 - 22.95)^2}{22.95}$$

$$= \frac{-2.19^2}{8.19} + \frac{3.23^2}{11.77} + \frac{-1.05^2}{24.05}$$

$$+ \frac{2.19^2}{7.81} + \frac{-3.23^2}{11.23} + \frac{1.05^2}{22.95}$$

$$= \frac{4.80}{8.19} + \frac{10.43}{11.77} + \frac{1.10}{24.05}$$

$$+ \frac{4.80}{7.81} + \frac{10.43}{11.23} + \frac{1.10}{22.95}$$

$$= .59(\text{Cell 1}) + .89 \,(\text{Cell 2})$$

$$+ .05(\text{Cell 3}) + .61(\text{Cell 4})$$

$$+ .93(\text{Cell 5}) + .05(\text{Cell 6})$$

$$= 3.12$$

3   Calculate the degrees of freedom from the formula:

$$df = (r - 1)(c - 1)$$

where

   r = number of rows in contingency Table 16

   c = number of columns in contingency Table 16

$r = 2$

$c = 3$

$$df = (2 - 1) \times (3 - 1) = 2$$

Looking up Significance in Table D

Table D gives critical values against which the observed value of χ^2 can be compared. The level of significance depends on the degrees of freedom (df). In our example, $df = 2$ so you should look along that row in Table D. Since our observed value of χ^2 is only 3.12, and so is less than the critical value of 5.99 for $p < .05$, the results of our experiment are not significant. We cannot reject the null hypothesis that any differences between the study patterns of social science and technology students are due to chance.

Since nominal categories are by definition unordered, it is not possible to make a one-tailed prediction about the direction of results in Table 16. A significant chi-square would simply tell you that overall there are differences between the observed frequencies of social science and technology students who fall into each of the study pattern categories. However, it is a good idea to insert the calculated values for each cell (shown in Step 2 of the step-by-step instructions) in Table 16. These values reflect the size of the difference between observed and expected frequencies for any particular cell, thus indicating the extent to which an actual observed frequency departs from what would be expected according to the null hypothesis. So cells which have the biggest values are those which have contributed most to any overall significant differences. For instance, as you can see from the values for each cell worked out in the step-by-step instructions, in Table 16 Cells 2 and 5 have the biggest values (.89 and .93). This means that there are significantly more social sciences students and significantly fewer technology students who have an irregular study pattern than would be expected by chance (i.e. in Cell 2 an actual observed frequency of 15 against an expected frequency of 11.77; and in Cell 5 an actual observed frequency of 8 against an expected frequency of 11.23).

A final reminder about using Table D is to check first that the *expected* frequencies for each cell are 5 or more. The calculated expected frequencies in our example (Step 1 of the step-by-step instructions) are all above 5. You could still have gone ahead if one of the expected frequencies in one cell had been under 5. But, if you find yourself with too many cells with expected frequencies under 5, you will have to use a different table of significance levels (known as the Fisher exact probability test) which you can find in a book by Siegel (1956). However, if you have around twenty subjects, and there is no reason to expect that the chance probabilities for each cell are likely to be odd in any way, you should be able to use the chi-square test.

Question 22

The study patterns of social science, technology and arts students were categorized as either regular or irregular. The results were as follows:
50 social science students: regular 25, irregular 25
45 technology students: regular 35, irregular 10
47 arts students: regular 20, irregular 27
Are these results significant? If so, at what level of significance?

Parametric Tests: An Introduction

With parametric tests it is possible to calculate proportions of total variability in scores which are due, on the one hand, to independent variables manipulated by the experimenter and, on the other, to unknown variables affecting subjects' performance.

7.1 PROPORTIONS OF VARIABILITY

This notion that total variability can be apportioned between different sources of variability is central to the use of parametric tests. As was pointed out in Chapter 3, Section 3.1, life for psychological researchers would be simple if *all* of the total variability in scores could be attributed to differences between experimental conditions as predicted by the experimental hypothesis. Unfortunately, human behaviour being what it is, there are always lots of unknown variables which are also producing differences in subjects' scores, such as individuals' abilities and motivations, different interpretations of the experimental task and so on.

If these unknown sources of variability are large they may mask any predicted differences in scores due to manipulation of the independent variables. So, as far as the researcher is concerned, variability due to variables *other* than those manipulated by the experimenter can be thought of as *error*. Thus total variability equals variability due to independent variables plus variability due to all other unknown variables.

Naturally, a researcher hopes that a *large* proportion of total variability in scores will be due to manipulation of independent variables while a relatively *small* proportion will be due to other variables (error). These proportions can be expressed as a *ratio*.

$$\frac{\text{predicted variability due to independent variables}}{\text{variability due to all other variables (error)}}$$

The higher this ratio, the greater the proportion of total variability is due to the independent variables and the less due to unknown variables. What we need to know is how high this ratio must be to allow us to say that our experimental results are significant, rather than due to unknown variability (error) as stated by the null hypothesis.

Parametric statistical tables give percentage probabilities of obtaining different values of these ratios. If a ratio is sufficiently large to be unlikely to have occurred by chance, the differences in scores can be considered as being significant. In other words, if the percentage probability of obtaining a particular ratio by chance is low ($p < .05$ or $p < .01$), the null hypothesis can be rejected and the results of the experiment can be interpreted as supporting the predictions made by the experimental hypothesis.

7.2 PARAMETRIC TESTS FOR ONE INDEPENDENT VARIABLE

These tests mirror the non-parametric tests described in Chapter 6. As you can see in the Decision Chart on the inside covers, all the tests for testing the significance of differences due to manipulation of *one* independent variable are grouped on the left-hand branch. As you follow through the various decision points you will find that each of the final boxes contains parallel parametric and non-parametric tests. We will be coming back to the question of when you should select a parametric test rather than an equivalent non-parametric test in Section 7.5.

Table 17 Parallel parametric and non-parametric tests for experimental designs with one independent variable

	Parametric test	Non-parametric test
Two experimental conditions with *same* (or *matched*) subjects	Related *t* test	Wilcoxon
Two experimental conditions with *different* subjects	Unrelated *t* test	Mann–Whitney
Three or more experimental conditions with *same* (or *matched*) subjects	One-way related ANOVA	Friedman Page's *L* Trend
Three or more experimental conditions with *different* subjects	One-way unrelated ANOVA	Kruskal–Wallis Jonckheere Trend Chi-square

7.3 PARAMETRIC TESTS FOR TWO OR MORE VARIABLES

You will have noticed in the Decision Chart on the inside covers the whole of the right-hand group of tests stemming from the *two or more variables* branch consists of parametric (ANOVA) tests. This is indeed where parametric tests really come into their own.

The point is that the rank ordering methods used in non-parametric tests only allows a comparison to be made between differences in ranks across conditions as a result of manipulating *one* independent variable. The great advantage of ANOVA tests is that exact proportions of variability in scores *can be attributed to any number of sources of variability.* In the variability ratio shown in Section 7.1 the proportion of variability due to all independent variables was amalgamated together on the top line to be compared with the proportion of error variability due to all other variables on the bottom line. But using ANOVA it is a simple matter to apportion out the proportions of variability due to each independent variable separately.

Before we go any further *it is essential that you reread Section 2.2 of Chapter 2* to remind yourself of the rationale for experimental designs in which two or more independent variables can be investigated simultaneously in the same experiment. As was made clear in that section, the main advantage of such experiments is that it is possible to test whether there is any *interaction* between the effects of different independent variables.

To follow up an example mentioned there, it might be important to know whether there is any interaction between success in absorbing the contents of different types of textbooks depending on the length of study periods allowed. Looking only at the main effect of using different textbooks might lead a researcher to come down in favour of textbook X. But the success of this book might depend crucially on how much study time students have available. Although textbook X might be fine for students who have plenty of study time, it might have been the other textbook Y that would have been more effective for students who can only study for short periods at a time.

Applying ANOVA to the results of an experiment with two or more variables tells you how much of the variability in scores is due to different sources of variability. In the above example this would be apportioned as follows:

(1) The main effect of the variable of textbook type (whether textbook X or textbook Y is studied).
(2) The main effect of the variable of study time (long or short study periods).
(3) The effect of the interaction between types of textbook and length of study periods.
(4) Effects due to all other unknown variables (error).

The initials ANOVA stand for *analysis of variance.* So far we have been talking about *variability* in scores. The statistical tests known collectively as analysis of variance (ANOVA) measure variability in terms of *variance.* Thus ANOVA enables you to calculate the amount of variance contributed by each possible *source of variance*; in the above example the variability due to the main effects (1) and (2), the interaction (3) and the error variance due to unknown variables (4).

In chapter 8 you will be given formulae which will enable you to calculate variance ratios for each of these sources of variance based on differences in subjects' scores in different experimental conditions. But once you have got the principle clear about how total variance is analysed between different sources of variance, there is nothing particularly difficult about the calculations.

PROGRESS BOX NINE

1   Analysis of variance (ANOVA) is a statistical technique for assessing the significance of experimental results. It does this by calculating from the scores in an experiment the proportions of total variance which are due to the independent variables and the interactions between them, and the proportion due to all other variables (error variance). These are known as F ratios.

2   The greater these F ratios the greater the proportion of variance which is due to the predicted effects of the independent variables and any interactions between them. The *lower* the F ratios, the greater the proportion of variance which is due to error, i.e. to unknown variables, as stated by the null hypothesis.

3   The statistical tables associated with ANOVA give percentage probabilities of obtaining high or low ratios. In general, for a given number of experimental conditions and subjects, the greater an F ratio the lower the probability that it is a chance result due to unknown variables.

4   Having looked up the percentage probabilities of getting the observed F ratios in your experiment, you can decide whether the probability of a chance result is low enough ($p < .05$ or $p < .01$) for you to reject the null hypothesis and accept that your experimental results support the experimental hypothesis.

7.4   REQUIREMENTS FOR PARAMETRIC TESTS

Because parametric tests make it possible to apportion exact variances from subjects' scores, there are special conditions specifying the kind of experimental data for which parametric tests are appropriate. With non-parametric tests it does not matter what your subjects' scores are as long as they can be ranked. A set of scores like 105, 104, 103, 100, 4, 3, 2 would still be ranked from 1 to 7. Non-parametric statistical tables would give you the same percentage probability for obtaining these ranks whether they are based on a bizarre set of scores like this or on a more usual range of scores like 10, 8, 7, 6, 4, 3, 3. Non-parametric tests are based on *ranks* and not on the actual numerical values of the scores themselves.

In contrast, parametric tests *are* based on exact numerical scores. Distributions of percentage probabilities in parametric statistical tables are based on certain mathematical variables known as *parameters* (hence the name parametric tests) which specify distributions of chance probabilities.

The data in your experiment have to be matched against the mathematical parameters which define these statistical distributions. The rationale is that unless your data meet these mathematical criteria any probabilities you read off from a parametric statistical table may be inaccurate. However, some statisticians have claimed that tests like ANOVA are in fact relatively 'robust'. What this means is that it is unlikely that percentage probabilities will be significantly inaccurate unless your data differs very markedly from the required conditions. But, if this *is* the case, then you will have to use an equivalent non-parametric test.

One requirement for calculating parametric 'statistics' is that it must be possible to carry out numerical calculations on your experimental data. It is not sufficient simply to be able to rank order the scores as with non-parametric tests. To meet this condition the scores from your experiment must be measured on at least an *interval scale* (see Chapter 2, Section 2.4). Strictly speaking, this means that parametric tests should be used only when the measures used are 'naturally' numerical, e.g. a continuous scale of reading times or numbers of items correctly recalled. However, as we have mentioned before, psychologists often allot numbers to all sorts of scales, for which it is simply *assumed* that there are equal intervals between the points on a continuous scale. Examples would be tests measuring reading ability, or the assessment of other people's behaviour using rating scales. The important thing for you to realize is that ANOVA should be carried out on scores which are on an interval scale, and try to make sure that any measures you use can at least be assumed to be numerical.

A second requirement is that scores should be *normally* distributed. Look back to the histogram of recall scores in Figure 1 in Chapter 3, Section 3.1. One point you will notice about such a distribution of scores is that there tend to be more scores in the middle range than at either end of the histogram. This is a very general characteristic of distributions of scores. Think about the heights of the adult population. You would expect to find more people in the middle range of heights (say 5–6 ft) than adults who are extremely tall (6–7 ft) or extremely short (3–4 ft).

Another characteristic feature of many distributions is that they are *symmetrical*. This means that there are equal numbers of scores on either side of the midpoint and that they fall off in a regular fashion to the left and right sides. Actually, the scores in the histogram in Figure 1 in Chapter 3, Section 3.1, are not distributed quite symmetrically because there is a tendency for there to be a greater bunching up of scores on the left side of the midpoint score of 5. But imagine a completely symmetrical distribution of scores, as shown in Figure 3. This time there are exactly equal numbers of scores arranged in a symmetrical pattern on either side of the midpoint.

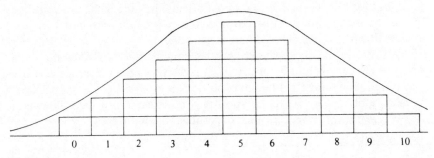

Figure 3

What the curved line in Figure 3 shows is a theoretical *normal distribution* for an infinite number of scores. However, it is important to realize that the continuous curve represents frequencies in exactly the same way as the squares in a histogram. With a histogram you can count up the exact frequencies of a finite number of scores. Since each square represents a score, the number of squares (i.e. the height of each column) tells you the frequency with which that score occurred. In exactly the same way the height of the distribution curve shows the frequencies of an infinite number of scores. The fact that the curve is tallest in the middle represents the fact that more scores are likely to occur in the middle range of scores while there are likely to be fewer extreme scores in the very short heights at the ends, or tails, of the distribution.

What you need to know is whether the scores in your experiment are *near* enough to being normally distributed to allow you to use parametric tests. One way of doing a rough check is to plot a distribution of all your scores in exactly the same way as was done in the histogram for the recall scores in Figure 1 in Chapter 3, Section 3.1. All you need to do is to plot the values of the possible scores in your experiment along the bottom and allot a square every time one of your subjects got that score. You can then see at a glance whether your total distribution of scores are roughly symmetrical around the midpoint. Because parametric tests are fairly 'robust', even when their assumptions are broken, you can go ahead with a parametric test unless your total distribution of scores looks very different from a normal distribution.

A third formal requirement for parametric tests is termed *homogeneity of variance*. What this means is that the variability of the scores in each condition should be approximately the *same*. Take again the example given at the beginning of this section and imagine that in an experiment with two conditions, the scores for Condition 1 are 105, 104, 103, 100, 4, 3, 2 and for Condition 2 10, 8, 7, 6, 4, 3, 3. It should be obvious that the range of variability in scores for these two conditions is noticeably different, the variability for Condition 1 being much larger. The idea is that it would be difficult to make comparisons between the two conditions based on the numerical values of scores as different as these.

Fortunately, it has been shown that, as long as there are *equal* numbers of subjects in each condition, it actually makes very little difference whether the variability in scores in different conditions is homogeneous (i.e. the same) or differs quite widely. So this is another good reason for always allocating the *same number of subjects* to each experimental condition.

PROGRESS BOX TEN

Requirements for parametric tests

1   There are three requirements for parametric tests.

    (a) Experimental scores are measured on an *interval scale*.

    (b) Scores are *normally distributed*.

    (c) The variability of scores for each experimental condition should be roughly the same, i.e. *homogeneity of variance*.

2   To test these assumptions it is essential that subjects' scores should be measured in a numerical form, even if this is not always based on a 'natural' interval scale. Plotting a histogram of all scores will give an indication of whether they have the roughly symmetrical shape of a normal distribution. Homogeneity of variance is not important as long as there are equal numbers of subjects in each experimental condition.

3   Parametric tests are reasonably 'robust' as far as these criteria are concerned; that is, unless your data are very divergent, you are unlikely to get seriously wrong answers about the percentage probabilities of obtaining the variance ratios in your experiment.

4   If your experimental data does differ a lot from any of these three parametric assumptions, you will have to use an equivalent non-parametric test, as shown in Table 17. In this case, you will have to test the effects of each independent variable *separately*; and therefore will not be able to look at the effects of any *interactions* between variables.

7.5 WHEN TO USE PARAMETRIC AND NON-PARAMETRIC TESTS

Let us stress once again that the function of both kinds of test is identical. In both cases an experimenter uses the tests to discover the probability that the results of his experiment occurred due to chance fluctuations caused by unknown variables. On the basis of this the researcher can decide whether this chance probability is low enough to warrant rejecting the null hypothesis and accepting the experimental hypothesis.

The difference between parametric and non-parametric tests concerns the method of calculating these chance probabilities. With the non-parametric tests in Chapter 6 this is done by rank ordering scores. If high or low ranks tend to occur in some conditions rather than others, this indicates that the scores are less likely to have occurred by chance but instead are due to predicted differences between experimental conditions.

However, it can be argued that the non-parametric method of putting scores into rank order is only measuring the variability in subjects' scores *indirectly*. Parametric tests, on the other hand, can measure the exact proportion of the total variability in scores which is due to differences between experimental conditions.

The argument is that this makes parametric tests more 'powerful' in the sense that they take into account more information about differences in scores. Ranking scores only puts them in order of magnitude, whereas parametric tests can use the actual numerical values of scores for calculating variances. This should make them more sensitive in picking up significant differences between subjects' performance in different experimental conditions.

However, there has been a lot of argument about this question of the relative power of tests among statisticians. Not all of them agree that parametric tests are all that more powerful than non-parametric tests. So on this basis alone there is no compelling reason against using the simpler non-parametric tests for analysing your data.

When you are deciding between parametric and non-parametric tests for dealing with only one independent variable as shown in Table 17, you have to weigh up the advantages of using a more sensitive parametric test as opposed to any problems you might encounter in trying to meet the requirements for applying parametric tests to your experimental data.

However, as we emphasized in Section 7.3, the major advantage of parametric tests is that they allow you to carry out an analysis of variance (ANOVA) on two or more independent variables simultaneously. In this way, a researcher is not confined to looking at the effects of single variables in isolation but can investigate interactions reflecting the combined effects of several independent variables.

PROGRESS BOX ELEVEN

When to use parametric and non-parametric tests:

	Advantages	*Disadvantages*
Parametric tests	1 They enable you to analyse interactions between *two or more* variables	1 The experimental data should meet the three requirements of interval measurement, normal distribution and homogeneity of variance (see Progress Box Nine) but also note the 'robustness' of parametric tests 2 The mathematical calculations are somewhat more complicated
Non-parametric tests	1 They can be used for investigating the effects of single variables when your experimental data do not meet the three requirements in Progress Box Nine, and they must be used when measurements are not numerical 2 They can be used to look at *trends* as well as overall differences between experimental conditions 3 Most of the calculations are easy and quick	1 Because non-parametric tests only look at the effects of single variables in isolation, they ignore a lot of the complexity of human behaviour 2 Because they make use of rank ordering rather than exact calculations of variance, they may have slightly less power in that they are less likely to pick up significant differences

CHAPTER 8

Parametric Tests: Step-by-Step

In this chapter we will be presenting parametric tests in the order shown below.

	Unrelated designs *(different subjects)*	*Related designs* *(same (or matched) subjects)*
One independent variable (two conditions)	1 *t* test (unrelated)	2 *t* test (related)
One independent variable (three or more conditions)	3 One-way ANOVA (unrelated)	4 One-way ANOVA (related)
Two independent variables (four or more conditions)	5 Two-way ANOVA (unrelated)	6 Two-way ANOVA (related)
	7 Two-way ANOVA (mixed unrelated and related)	
	8 Extensions of ANOVA	

Note that for parametric tests we will be giving you the tests for *unrelated* designs first, because these are on the whole easier to calculate. This does *not* apply, however, to the very first test, the unrelated *t* test. We often tell students that this is the 'worst' calculation of all. If you can keep your head and work through the various parts of this formula in the correct order, all subsequent calculations will seem like child's play.

The *t* tests are differentiated from ANOVA for several reasons. First, they can only be used for testing differences between *two* conditions when only *one* variable is being manipulated, whereas ANOVA can be extended to cover cases when several conditions are used to test two or more variables. The *t* test can be used when numbers of subjects are quite small and the table of percentage probabilities for the *t* test have been calculated on this basis. Because psychologists often test differences between two conditions using quite small numbers of subjects, t tests are among the most frequently used parametric tests. However, the basic idea of comparing variances due to independent variables against total variance is common to both the t tests and ANOVA.

When you come to tackling ANOVA, it would probably be a good idea to start with one-way ANOVA (unrelated) which is the simplest of all. Two-way ANOVA (unrelated) is also much easier to grasp than two-way ANOVA (related). So you should have a go at the two-way ANOVA (unrelated) before trying either the two-way ANOVA (related) or the two-way ANOVA (mixed).

The information given for each parametric test is divided into six parts.

(1) *When to use.* This reminds you of appropriate experimental designs for using the test.
(2) *Example.* This gives a sample set of data to be analysed.
(3) For ANOVA tests a *sources of variance table.* This includes the appropriate variances for the independent variables, interactions and error, and F ratios.
(4) *Rationale.* In this section you will be told the rationale for using particular methods for calculating variances.
(5) *Step-by-step instructions.* This section takes you through the calculations, giving formulae in the most convenient order for carrying out the calculations.
(6) *Looking up significance in tables.* This section gives precise instructions about how to look up the significance of t tests and F ratios in the appropriate statistical tables.

Note about calculations

As we pointed out earlier, the calculations for parametric tests are—if not all that more difficult—at least much more laborious than those for non-parametric tests. The main type of calculation, with which you will soon become all too familiar, is to square a lot of numbers and then add up the total of these squares. As long as you have a pocket calculator with a memory and an M + or sum facility there is a very simple method for doing this. Simply square each number and accumulate it into memory.

As with the calculations for the non-parametric tests, you may find that your answers differ from ours in the last decimal place, depending on whether intermediate figures have been rounded up. Obviously, such slight differences do not matter.

8.1 THE *t* TEST (UNRELATED)

When to Use

The unrelated *t* test is used for experimental designs with *two* conditions testing *one* independent variable, when *different* subjects are doing the two conditions (an *unrelated* design).

The unrelated *t* test is the parametric equivalent of the non-parametric Mann–Whitney test for *unrelated* designs with *two* experimental conditions.

Example

One group of ten subjects were given a simple text to read and another group of ten subjects a complex text (Table 18). It was predicted that more words would be recalled from the simple text.

Table 18 Number of words recalled from a simple text and a complex text

	Group 1 (simple text)		Group 2 (complex text)	
	Scores (x_1)	Squared scores (x_1^2)	Scores (x_2)	Squared scores (x_2^2)
	10	100	2	4
	5	25	1	1
	6	36	7	49
	3	9	4	16
	9	81	4	16
	8	64	5	25
	7	49	2	4
	5	25	5	25
	6	36	3	9
	5	25	4	16
Total	$\sum x_1$ 64	$\sum x_1^2$ 450	$\sum x_2$ 37	$\sum x_2^2$ 165
Mean	M_1 6.4		M_2 3.7	

Rationale

The basic aim of the unrelated *t* test is to compare the amount of variability due to the predicted differences in scores between the two groups as against the total variability in subjects' scores. The predicted differences are calculated as a difference between the mean scores for the two groups. The actual value of this difference between the means has to be compared against the overall range and variability in scores. If there is only a little variability in the scores, then quite a small difference between the means might reflect a consistent difference between the groups. However, if there is a lot of variability indicating a wide range of scores, this might indicate that more of the variability is due to fluctuations in individuals' performance due to unknown variables rather than to the predicted difference between the conditions.

Total variance in scores is measured by a formula which takes into account the variability in individual scores around the mean. It does this by adding up the individual scores (squared) and subtracting the mean (also squared); in other words, by working out how much each individual score *deviates* from the mean.

What makes this somewhat complicated for the unrelated t test is that this total variance has to be calculated by combining the variances calculated for each group of subjects separately. The horrendous-looking formula given in step 5 of the step-by-step instructions shows the differences between the group means on the top line. Below the line the separate variances for each group are calculated, added together and divided by the combined degrees of freedom for each group of subjects (see Chapter 4, Section 4.3.1). Finally, you have to take the square root of the total variance so that it can be directly compared against the absolute value of the difference between the means. All this will seem less formidable (we hope!) as you work your way through the formula.

The statistic t represents the size of the difference between the means for the two groups, taking total variance into account. In order to be significant the observed value of t has to be *equal* to or *larger* than the critical values of t given in Table H.

Step-by-Step instructions for Calculating (unrelated) t

1	Square each individual score for both groups separately	See columns in Table 18 for *Squared scores* (x_1^2) and *Squared scores* (x_2^2)
2	Add up the totals of scores and squared scores for each group. Note the symbol $\sum$ means to *sum* the individual scores (x_1) and (x_2) and the squared scores (x_1^2) and (x_2^2)	$\sum x_1 = 64$ $\sum x_2 = 37$ $\sum x_1{}^2 = 450$ $\sum x_2{}^2 = 165$

3   Square the totals of individual scores for each group (note the difference between $(\sum x)^2$ for which you add up the scores first and *then* square the total and $\sum x^2$ for which you square the individual scores first and then add them up)

$(\sum x_1)^2 = 64 \times 64 = 4096$
$(\sum x_2)^2 = 37 \times 37 = 1369$

4   Calculate the means for each group

$M_1 = 6.4, M_2 = 3.7$

5   Find the value of t from the formula:

$$t = \frac{M_1 - M_2}{\sqrt{\dfrac{\left(\sum x_1^2 - \dfrac{(\sum x_1)^2}{n_1}\right) + \left(\sum x_2^2 - \dfrac{(\sum x_2)^2}{n_2}\right)}{(n_1 - 1) + (n_2 - 1)}\left(\dfrac{1}{n_1} + \dfrac{1}{n_2}\right)}}$$

where

M_1 = mean for Group 1	$M_1 = 6.4$
M_2 = mean for Group 2	$M_2 = 3.7$
$\sum x_1^2$ = sum of squares for Group 1	$\sum x_1^2 = 450$
$\sum x_2^2$ = sum of squares for Group 2	$\sum x_2^2 = 165$
$(\sum x_1)^2$ = squared total of scores for Group 1	$(\sum x_1)^2 = 4096$
$(\sum x_2)^2$ = squared total of scores for Group 2	$(\sum x_2)^2 = 1369$
n_1 = number of subjects in Group 1	$n_1 = 10$
n_2 = number of subjects in Group 2	$n_2 = 10$

$$t = \cfrac{6.4 - 3.7}{\sqrt{\cfrac{\left(450 - \cfrac{4096}{10}\right) + \left(165 - \cfrac{1369}{10}\right)}{9 + 9}\left(\cfrac{1}{10} + \cfrac{1}{10}\right)}}$$

$$= \cfrac{2.7}{\sqrt{\cfrac{450 - 409.6 + 165 - 136.9}{18} \times \cfrac{1}{5}}}$$

$$= \cfrac{2.7}{\sqrt{3.806 \times .2}}$$

$$= \cfrac{2.7}{\sqrt{.7612}}$$

$$= \cfrac{2.7}{.872}$$

$$= 3.096$$

(N.B. It does not matter whether subtracting M_2 from M_1 results in a plus or minus number. When you are looking up the value of t, you simply ignore the sign).

6 Calculate the degrees of freedom i.e. the number of subjects in each condition minus one added together
$$df = (n_1 - 1) + (n_2 - 1)$$
$$= (10 - 1) + (10 - 1)$$
$$= 18$$

Looking up Significance of t in Table H

We look down the left-hand column to find the df (in our example 18). Then we look along the row to see whether the observed value of t (in our example 3.096) is *larger* than or *equal* to the critical values. Depending on whether we have made a one-tailed hypothesis that the difference in means would go in one direction, or a two-tailed hypothesis that the difference would go in either direction, we can read off the appropriate significance level. In our example, the observed t value of 3.096 is larger than the critical value of 2.878, indicating a significance level of $p < .005$ for a one-tailed hypothesis or $p < .01$ for a two-tailed hypothesis. Note that when there is no entry for your exact df, you should use the next lowest df, as indicated in the footnote to the table.

8.2 THE *t* TEST (RELATED)

When to Use

The related test is used for experimental designs with *two* conditions testing *one* independent variable, when the *same* (or matched) subjects are doing both conditions (a *related* design).

The related test is the parametric equivalent of the non-parametric Wilcoxon test for *related* designs with *two* experimental conditions.

Example

Ten subjects were each given two types of text to read, a simple text and a complex text (Table 19). The experimenter predicted that more words would be recalled from the simple text.

Table 19 Number of words recalled from a simple text and a complex text

Subject	Condition A (simple text)	Condition B (complex text)	d $(A - B)$	d^2
1	10	2	8	64
2	5	1	4	16
3	6	7	− 1	1
4	3	4	− 1	1
5	9	4	5	25
6	8	5	3	9
7	7	2	5	25
8	5	5	0	0
9	6	3	3	9
10	5	4	1	1
Total	64	37	$\sum d = 27$	$\sum d^2 = 151$
Mean	6.4	3.7		

Rationale

As with the unrelated *t* test, the aim is to compare the predicted differences between the two experimental conditions against the total variability in the scores. When there were different subjects in each condition it was only possible to compare the means for the two groups. When the *same* subjects are used for both conditions, it becomes possible to compare pairs of scores obtained by each individual subject when performing under the two conditions. The same applies if pairs of subjects are matched on all relevant characteristics. As with the unrelated t these differences in scores are compared against the total variance in the differences between scores, calculated by adding the squares of the differences in scores and dividing them by the degrees of freedom.

The statistic t represents the size of the differences between subjects' scores for the two conditions. In order to be significant the observed value of t has to be *equal* to or *larger* than the critical values of t in Table H.

Step-by-Step Instructions for Calculating (related) t

1   Calculate the differences between subjects' scores by subtracting Condition B scores from Condition A

See column $d(A - B)$ in Table 19

2   Square these differences

See column d^2

3   Add up the differences (counting minus scores as minuses) and the squared differences (note symbol $\sum$ = to *sum*)

$\sum d = 27$

$\sum d^2 = 151$

4   Square the total of differences (note difference between $(\sum d)^2$, i.e. add up the differences and then square the total, and $\sum d^2$, i.e. square the differences and then add them up)

$(\sum d)^2 = 27 \times 27 = 729$

5   Find t from the formula

$$t = \frac{\sum d}{\sqrt{\dfrac{N \sum d^2 - (\sum d)^2}{N - 1}}}$$

$$t = \frac{27}{\sqrt{\dfrac{10 \times 151 - (27)^2}{10 - 1}}}$$

where

$\sum d$ = sum of differences between A and B scores

$$= \frac{27}{\sqrt{\dfrac{1510 - 729}{9}}}$$

$\sum d^2$ = sum of squared differences

$(\sum d)^2$ = sum of differences squared

$$= \frac{27}{\sqrt{86.78}}$$

N = number of subjects

$\sqrt{}$ = take the square root

$$= \frac{27}{9.315}$$
$$= 2.89$$

6   Calculate the degrees of freedom, $df = N - 1 = 10 - 1 = 9$
i.e. number of subjects (N) minus
one

Looking up Significance of t in Table H

We look down the left-hand column and find the degrees of freedom (in our example 9). If the observed value of t is *larger* than or *equal* to a critical value in that row we can reject the null hypothesis at that particular level of significance. In our example the observed t value of 2.89 is larger than the critical value of 2.821 at the significance level of $p < .01$ (one-tailed) or $p < .02$ (two-tailed).

Question 23

Analyse the data given below assuming that two groups of *different* subjects were allocated to condition A and condition B.

(a) Are the results significant? If so, at what level of significance for a *one-tailed* hypothesis?
(b) Now imagine that all the scores came from the *same* subjects doing both conditions. What is the observed value of t? Is it significant? If so at what level of significance for a *two-tailed* hypothesis?

Condition A	Condition B
6	2
7	1
8	3
10	4
8	3
8	2
5	7
3	4

8.3   GENERAL METHOD FOR ANOVA

As was pointed out in Chapter 7, Analysis of Variance (ANOVA) really comes into its own when there are several experimental conditions testing the effects of two or more independent variables. When there are two or more variables the aim is to break down the variance due to independent variables into the variance due to each variable separately and to any interactions between variables. In each case, the variance due to each variable must be compared against the error variance, i.e. the variance due to all other unknown variables. Thus one ends up with a separate F ratio for *each* source of variability. The greater an F ratio the more likely it is that the variability in scores due to that variable is significant (see Chapter 7, Section 7.1).

Table 20   ANOVA table

Source of variance	F ratios
Variable A (textbook X or Y)	$\dfrac{\text{variance due to variable A}}{\text{error variance}}$
Variable B (short or long study periods)	$\dfrac{\text{variance due to variable A}}{\text{error variance}}$
Interaction A × B	$\dfrac{\text{variance due to interaction A × B}}{\text{error variance}}$
Error variance	
Total variance	

All this will probably become much clearer if you look at Table 20. This shows how an ANOVA table can be drawn up, showing each source of variance and its associated F ratio. This table expresses the fact that all sources of variability must add up to the total variability in subjects' scores. It also shows that F ratios can be calculated for each source of variance separately. You can probably see by now that the reason this statistical technique is called analysis of variance (ANOVA) is because it provides a method for calculating the amounts of variance due to all possible sources of variability in subjects' scores. If you think about it, what we are doing is to apportion, or *analyse*, the total amount of variance into its component parts.

Question 24

Draw up an ANOVA table showing sources of variance for an experiment in which two groups of children, poor spellers and good spellers, are exposed to two different reading schemes: Scheme 1 and Scheme 2.

Obviously what is needed are formulae which will enable you to calculate each of these variances. For ANOVA it is necessary to calculate separate variances for each source of variance, including the error variance. As with the t test, the basic method is to sum squares of individual scores, subtract the square of the mean and divide by the appropriate degrees of freedom. So you will find that ANOVA formulae contain many examples of the symbol

$\sum$ (to *sum*) followed by an indication of which squared scores and totals should be summed. As you become familiar with the technique it will become increasingly clear which scores contribute to the calculation of which sources of variance.

8.3.1   Sums of Squares

The first step is to calculate the *sums of squares* (*SS*) for each source of variance. Full instructions about how to do this will be given in the remaining sections of this chapter. When calculating sums of squares, it is useful to remember that the *SS* for all the variables, interactions and error *must add up to the total variance*. In fact, the *SS* for the error variance is calculated by subtracting all the other sources of variance from the total variance.

8.3.2   Degrees of Freedom

The next step when drawing up an ANOVA table is to work out the degrees of freedom. Look back now to Section 4.3.1 of Chapter 4 which explains the underlying rationale of degrees of freedom. The basic idea is that when all other scores are known the last one is *not free to vary*. So the degrees of freedom to vary are calculated as $N - 1$. Exactly the same applies when one is looking at experimental conditions. If there are three conditions and you already know the total scores for two of these conditions and the overall total score, the total score for the third condition can be calculated; that is, it is predictable on the basis of this information and so is *not free to vary*.

For each independent variable there are a number of experimental conditions which are used to test that variable. So the relevant degrees of freedom for each variable are the number of conditions minus one ($C - 1$). The degrees of freedom for the total variance is calculated from the total number of scores minus one ($N - 1$). Other degrees of freedom for interactions and error are calculated by multiplying and subtracting these basic degrees of freedom, as shown in Progress Box Twelve.

To demonstrate how this works, let us expand the ANOVA table in Table 20 to show all the columns which need to be filled in (Table 21). Note that there are *twenty* subjects and that there are *two* conditions for variable *A* (textbook X or textbook Y) and *two* conditions for variable *B* (short or long study periods).

Following the rules given in Progress Box Twelve, check the allocation of degrees of freedom (*df*) to the different sources of variance in Table 21.

PROGRESS BOX TWELVE

1 The *df* (degrees of freedom) for each independent variable is calculated by subtracting one from the number of conditions used to test that variable.

2 The *df* for interactions is calculated by multiplying the *df* of the relevant variables together.

3 The *df* for the total variance is calculated by subtracting one from the total number of scores produced by all the subjects.

4 The *df* for the error variance is calculated by subtracting the *df* for all the variables and interactions from the total *df*. It is for this reason that error is sometimes known as *residual error*, i.e. what is 'left over' after all the other variances and *df* have been calculated.

5 You will need *df* for dividing the sums of squares to arrive at mean square variances; and also when you come to look up the significance of *F* ratios in the appropriate statistical table.

Table 21 ANOVA table

Source of variance	Sums of Squares (SS)	Degrees of freedom (df)	Mean squares (MS)	F ratios
Variable *A* (textbook X or Y)		$2 - 1 = 1$		
Variable *B* (short or long study periods)		$2 - 1 = 1$		
Interaction $A \times B$		$1 \times 1 = 1$		
Error variance		$19 - 1 - 1 - 1 = 16$		
Total variance		$20 - 1 = 19$		

8.3.3 Mean Squares

In order to arrive at the mean squares (*MS*) it is necessary to divide each sum of squares (*SS*) by the appropriate degrees of freedom (*df*). It is the mean squares (*MS*) which represent the calculated amount of variance attributable to each source of variance. Note that these mean square measures of variance for all the sources of variance do *not* add up to the total variance. This is because they have been divided by different degrees of freedom for each source of variance.

Looking back to Table 20, the *F* ratio for each source of variance is the ratio of that particular variance divided by the error variance. Since the mean squares (MS) represent measures of variance, the F ratio for each variable is the MS for that variable over the MS for the error variance.

So for variable A the F ratio is:

$$\frac{MS(\text{variable } A)}{MS(\text{error})}$$

For variable B the F ratio is:

$$\frac{MS(\text{variable } B)}{MS(\text{error})}$$

For the interaction $A \times B$ the F ratio is:

$$\frac{MS(\text{interaction } A \times B)}{MS(\text{error})}$$

In order to look up the significance of an F ratio we also need to know the degrees of freedom associated with these mean squares. So for the F ratio for variable A in Table 21 we write:

$$F_{1,16} = \frac{MS(\text{variable } A)}{MS(\text{error})}$$

These subscripts for $F_{1,16}$ indicate that in Table 21 the df for variable A is 1 and the df for the error variance is 16. The df for the F ratios for variable B and for the interaction $A \times B$ are also both $F_{1,16}$ (see Table 21).

The final step is to look up these F ratios in Table I. Using the df for each variable and the df for the error variance, you can compare the observed F ratios obtained in your experiment against the percentage probabilities that the differences between conditions are a chance result due to error variance, as stated by the null hypothesis.

8.3.4 Preparing Data for ANOVA

The usual way of presenting the scores for an ANOVA experimental design with two independent variables is in a 2×2 table. Table 22 gives the results of the textbook experiment, in which twenty subjects were allocated five to each of the following four conditions.

Textbook X with short study periods
Textbook X with long study periods
Textbook Y with short study periods
Textbook Y with long study periods

In Table 22, each square shows the individual scores for five subjects and the total for each group.

Table 22 Two by two table for an ANOVA design with two
independent variables

Variable B (length of study periods)	Variable A (type of text) Textbook X		Textbook Y		Totals B
Short study periods	4 3 6 8 7	28	5 4 7 2 8	26	54
Long study periods	8 9 8 7 10	42	5 2 3 4 7	21	63
Totals A		70		47	117 Grand total

A 2×3 table might include three types of text, which would give you six
squares of scores. A 3×3 table would have nine squares, and so on. In
all these cases you would have to calculate the total scores for each group,
the row and column totals, and the grand total.

It is very important to note that the score for each subject in any one
condition (square) of an ANOVA table represents a single score from that
subject. So, if you have taken several measures from each subject under
each condition, you should work out a mean score for each subject and
insert it in the table. If you are using a *same subjects* related design, then, of
course, you need to have one mean score for each subject for each of the
conditions he or she has done. If the scores in Table 22 had been obtained
from only five subjects, all of whom had done all four conditions, then
for each subject you would have four scores to be inserted in each of the
four squares in the table.

A final point to notice is that all the ANOVA calculations we shall be
dealing with assume that there are *equal numbers* of subjects in each condition.
The formulae for dealing with equal numbers are much simpler than when
there are unequal numbers of subjects in each condition. So you should
always try to arrange your experiment so that you test equal numbers
of subjects in each condition. In fact, all the ANOVA formulae given in
this chapter are suitable only for designs with equal numbers of subjects
in each condition.

We can now draw up an ANOVA table showing for each source of variance,
including error variance, the sums of squares (*SS*) and the degrees of freedom

(df). When we divide each SS by the df we obtain the measure of variance known as the mean square (MS). For each source of variance, an F ratio can be calculated comparing the MS variance for each independent variable against the error variance, and allocating the appropriate df for the variable and for the error. The larger an F ratio is, the more significant is the proportion of variance due to that independent variable as compared with the error variance due to all other unknown variables. The full ANOVA table for the textbook experiment shown in Table 22 is given in Table 23.

Table 23   Full ANOVA table

Source of variance	Sums of squares (SS)	Degrees of freedom (df)	Mean squares (MS)	F ratios
Variable A (textbook X or Y)	SS	1	$\dfrac{SS}{1}$	$F_{1,16}\dfrac{MS(A)}{MS(\text{error})}$
Variable B (short or long study periods)	SS	1	$\dfrac{SS}{1}$	$F_{1,16}\dfrac{MS(B)}{MS(\text{error})}$
Interaction $A \times B$	SS	1	$\dfrac{SS}{1}$	$F_{1,16}\dfrac{MS(A \times B)}{MS(\text{error})}$
Error	SS	16	$\dfrac{SS}{16}$	
Total	SS	19		

Question 25

An experiment was carried out to investigate recall scores for lists of meaningful words or nonsense syllables (variable A) depending on whether the items were presented at a fast, medium or slow rate of presentation (variable B). There were thirty subjects, five of whom were allocated to each experimental condition.

(a) Draw a 2 × 3 table to show the six experimental conditions.
(b) Draw up an ANOVA table filling in the relevant degrees of freedom (df) and the formulae for mean squares and F ratios as shown in Table 23. Note that there are *three* conditions for variable B (see Progress Box Twelve).

In the remaining sections of this chapter we will be presenting ANOVA calculations for different types of experimental design, depending on how many variables and experimental conditions are being investigated. We shall be starting with the simplest case in which there is only *one* variable. You will remember that t tests can only be used when there are *two* experimental conditions. When an experimenter wants to set up three or more experimental conditions to test several levels of one variable, it is necessary to use a *one-way* ANOVA. Two-way ANOVAs of the kind we have been discussing are needed when the effects of at least *two or more* variables are being investigated in a single experiment.

PROGRESS BOX THIRTEEN

How to carry out analysis of variance (ANOVA):

1 Present the scores in your experiment in an appropriate table (2×2, 2×3, etc.).
2 Discuss whether your experimental scores meet the three parametric assumptions listed in Progress Box Ten (Chapter 7, Section 7.4).
3 Draw up an ANOVA sources of variance table, showing the variances for each variable, any interactions, the error variance and the total variance.
4 Calculate the sums of squares (SS), degrees of freedom (df) and mean squares (MS) for each source of variance.
5 Calculate the F ratios for each source of variance, i.e. the MS for each independent variable and interaction over the MS error of variance. For each F ratio indicate the appropriate df for the variable and the df for the error.
6 Look up the F ratios in Table I to discover the probability that your results could be a chance result due to error variance, as stated by the null hypothesis. If this probability is below 5% or 1%, reject the null hypothesis, and accept that your results are significant at the $p < .05$ or $p < .01$ significance level.

8.4 ONE-WAY ANOVA (UNRELATED)

When to use

This analysis is used when *one* variable is tested under *three or more* conditions and *different* subjects are used for each of the conditions.

The one-way unrelated ANOVA is the parametric equivalent of the non-parametric Kruskal–Wallis test for *unrelated* designs with *three or more* conditions.

Example

Three different groups of six subjects were given lists of ten words to learn, the first group at a slow rate of one word every 5 sec, the second group at a medium rate of one word every 2 s and the third group at a fast rate of one word every 1 s. It was predicted that recall scores would be affected by rate of presentation. The results are shown in Table 24.

Table 24   Table of results: number of words recalled

	Group 1 (slow rate)	Group 2 (medium rate)	Group 3 (fast rate)	
	8	7	4	
	7	8	5	
	9	5	3	
	5	4	6	
	6	6	2	
	8	7	4	
Total (T_c)	43	37	24	104 Grand total
Mean	7.17	6.17	4	

Sources of Variance Table

For a one-way *unrelated* design the source of variance table is simple because only one independent variable is being tested (Table 25).

Table 25   Sources of variance table for one-way unrelated design

Source of variance	Sums of squares (SS)	Degrees of freedom (df)	Mean squares (MS)	F ratios
Presentation rate variable (between conditions)	SS_{bet}	df_{bet}	$\dfrac{SS_{bet}}{df_{bet}}$	$\dfrac{MS_{bet}}{MS_{error}}$
Error	SS_{error}	df_{error}	$\dfrac{SS_{error}}{df_{error}}$	
Total	SS_{tot}	df_{tot}		

Rationale

The presentation rate variable represents the predicted differences in recall scores *between* the conditions of words being presented at a slow, medium or fast rate. In an unrelated design, when different groups of subjects are doing the different conditions, any differences in scores between conditions are also differences between groups of subjects. However, any differences between subjects *within* each group of subjects doing each condition must be due to other irrelevant variables, whether these are individual differences between subjects or uncontrolled variables causing them to react in different ways. The F ratio represents a test of the experimental hypothesis that the variance *between* conditions will be relatively large compared with the error variance *within* each group of subjects doing each condition.

We shall be calculating the sum of squares for each source of variance by adding together the squared scores for the appropriate differences between and within conditions. In each case, we have to subtract a *constant* mean value from each sum of squares.

For SS_{bet} we need to add up the squares of the totals for the experimental conditions in order to calculate the predicted variance in subjects' scores as a result of differences between the conditions.

For SS_{tot} we add up the squares of all the individual scores since these represent the total variability in subjects' scores.

The SS_{error} represents all the variability in scores 'left-over' after the variability due to experimental conditions (SS_{bet}) has been subtracted from total variability (SS_{tot}).

The appropriate *degrees of freedom* (df) are calculated in a similar way. The df for SS_{bet} are the number of conditions minus one. The df for SS_{tot} are the total number of subjects' scores minus one. And the df for SS_{error} are obtained by subtracting the df_{bet} from the total df (see Progress Box Twelve).

The F ratio for between conditions represents the size of the variance due to the experimental conditions in relation to error variance. To be significant the observed value of the statistic F has to be *equal* to or *larger* than the critical values in Table I.

Step-by-Step Instructions for Calculating the Value of F

Calculate SS from the following formulae (using the scores in Table 24) where

$\sum T_c^2$ = sum of the squared totals for each condition $\sum T_c^2 = 43^2 + 37^2 + 24^2$

n = number of subjects in each condition $n = 6$

N = total number of scores $N = 18$

$(\sum x)^2$ = grand total squared $(\sum x)^2 = 104^2$

$\dfrac{(\sum x^2)}{N}$ = *constant* to be subtracted from all SS

x = each individual score

$\sum x^2$ = sum of squared individual scores

Note the difference between $\sum x^2$, when all the individual scores are first squared and then added up, and $(\sum x)^2$, when individual scores are first added up to make a grand total, which is then squared. Also note that all these formulae apply only when there are *equal* numbers of subjects in each condition and we are assuming this throughout.

1   Calculate SS_{bet} from the formula

$$\frac{\sum T_c^2}{n} - \frac{(\sum x)^2}{N}$$

$$SS_{bet} = \frac{43^2 + 37^2 + 24^2}{6} - \frac{104^2}{18}$$

$$= \frac{3794}{6} - \frac{10816}{18}$$

$$= 632.33 - 600.89$$

$$= 31.44$$

2   Calculate SS_{tot} from the formula

$$\sum x^2 - \frac{(\sum x)^2}{N}$$

$$SS_{tot} = 8^2 + 7^2 + 9^2 + 5^2 + 6^2$$
$$+ 8^2 + 7^2 + 8^2 + 5^2 + 4^2$$
$$+ 6^2 + 7^2 + 4^2 + 5^2 + 3^2$$
$$+ 6^2 + 2^2 + 4^2 - \frac{104^2}{18}$$

$$= 664 - \frac{10816}{18}$$

$$= 664 - 600.89$$

$$= 63.11$$

3   Calculate SS_{error} from the formula
    $SS_{tot} - SS_{bet}$

$SS_{error} = 63.11 - 31.44$
$\quad\quad = 31.67$

4   Calculate the degrees of freedom
    df_{bet} = number of conditions $- 1$
    $df_{tot} = N - 1$
    $df_{error} = df_{tot} - df_{bet}$

$df_{bet} = 3 - 1 = 2$
$df_{tot} = 18 - 1 = 17$
$df_{error} = 17 - 2 = 15$

5   Divide each SS by df to obtain MS

$$MS_{bet} = \frac{SS_{bet}}{df_{bet}}$$

$$MS_{bet} = \frac{31.44}{2} = 15.72$$

$$MS_{error} = \frac{SS_{error}}{df_{error}}$$

$$MS_{error} = \frac{31.67}{15} = 2.11$$

6   Calculate the F ratio for MS_{bet}
    over MS_{error}, allocating the cor-
    rect df to (MS_{bet}) and (MS_{error})

$$F \text{ ratio for } MS_{bet} = \frac{MS_{bet}}{MS_{error}} \qquad\qquad F_{2, 15} = \frac{15.72}{2.11} = 7.45$$

7   Complete the ANOVA table in
    Table 26

Table 26   ANOVA table

Source of variance	Sums of squares (SS)	Degrees of freedom (df)	Mean squares (MS)	F ratios
Presentation rate	31.44	2	15.72	$F_{2,15} = 7.45$
Error	31.67	15	2.11	
Total	63.11	17		

Looking up Significance in Tables I(1)–(4)

To look up the significance of the observed value of F we always use the same set of tables: Table I(1)–(4). Each of these four tables gives the critical value of F for four different levels of significance. Table I(1) shows the critical values of F at the $p < .05$ level; Table I(2) at the $p < .025$ level; Table I(3) at the $p < .01$ level; and Table I(4) at the $p < .001$ level.

   We need to know the degrees of freedom to locate the critical value of F in the table. With our worked example we look up F as follows. The two degrees of freedom that we use are the df_{bet} and the df_{error} (2 and 15, respectively). In Table I(1) the df_{bet} is shown along the v_1 row and df_{error} is shown down the v_2 column. All we do, therefore, is to locate 2 on the v_1 row and follow the v_2 column down until we find 15. In Table I(1) the critical value of $F_{2, 15}$ is 3.68 for $p < .05$ level of significance. Since the observed value of F is 7.45, and therefore larger than 3.68, we can reject the null hypothesis and conclude that rate of presentation has a significant effect on recall of words. Note that the df for the variable is always v_1 and the df for the error is always v_2.

   The next step is to see whether the observed value of F is significant at the levels of significance given in Tables I(2)–(4). Our observed F value of 7.45 is significant at the $p < .025$ and $p < .01$ levels of significance, since the critical values of $F_{2, 15}$ at these levels in Tables I(2) and (3) are 4.76 and 6.36, respectively. However, it is not significant at the $p < .001$ level of significance because our observed value of 7.45 is smaller than the critical value for $F_{2,15}$ of 11.34 in Table I(4).

One thing you should note is that we can only say that there are some differences in recall scores for slow, medium and fast presentation rates. If you look back to the totals for the three conditions in Table 24 you will see that it looks as if the significant differences are due to the score for Condition 3 being considerably smaller than those for Conditions 1 and 2. To check whether this is statistically significant you might want to carry out the non-parametric Jonckheere trend test for unrelated designs (see Chapter 6, Section 6.6).

Question 26

Variable A		
A_1	A_2	
4	3	
8	2	
7	1	
6	4	Grand
5	7	total
30	17	47

(a) Analyse the above data using a one-way *unrelated* ANOVA design. Follow the step-by-step instructions for calculating the formulae and filling in an ANOVA table.
(b) Are the results significant at any of the levels of significance in Tables I(1)–(4)?
(c) Calculate ANOVA for the following data. Before you start make a guess what the variances will turn out to be.

A_1	A_2	A_3	A_4	
10	10	10	10	
10	10	10	10	
10	10	10	10	
10	10	10	10	
10	10	10	10	Grand
				total
50	50	50	50	200

8.5 ONE-WAY ANOVA (RELATED)

When to Use

This analysis is used when *one* variable is tested under *three or more* conditions and the *same* (or *matched*) subjects are used for all experimental conditions.

The one-way related ANOVA is the parametric equivalent of the non-parametric Friedman test for a *related* design with *three or more* conditions.

Example

We are going to use the same experimental results as in Section 8.4. But this time we assume that the *same* six subjects are doing all three experimental conditions, learning different lists of words under slow, medium and fast rates of presentation. The results are shown in Table 27. Notice that this time there are three scores for each subject. We have added up the totals for each condition, the totals for each subject and the grand total of all the scores (104).

Table 27   Table of results: number of words recalled

Subject	Condition 1 (slow rate)	Condition 2 (medium rate)	Condition 3 (fast rate)	Total for subjects (T_s)	
1	8	7	4	19	
2	7	8	5	20	
3	9	5	3	17	
4	5	4	6	15	
5	6	6	2	14	
6	8	7	4	19	
Total (T_c)	43	37	24	104	Grand total

Sources of Variance Table

For a one-way *related* design the ANOVA table is a bit more complicated than for an unrelated design (see Table 28).

Rationale

Again the presentation rate variable 'between conditions' represents the predicted differences in recall scores between the three experimental conditions. However, this time *between conditions* is not the same as *between subjects*. Since all the subjects are doing all three conditions, it is possible to look at the overall performance of each of the six subjects across all three conditions. This means that the differences in scores due to individual subjects can be treated as a separate source of variance.

Table 28 Sources of variance table for one way related design

Source of variance	Sums of squares (SS)	Degrees of freedom (df)	Mean squares (MS)	F ratios
Presentation rate variable (between conditions)	SS_{bet}	df_{bet}	$\dfrac{SS_{bet}}{df_{bet}}$	$\dfrac{MS_{bet}}{MS_{error}}$
Subjects	SS_{subj}	df_{subj}	$\dfrac{SS_{subj}}{df_{subj}}$	$\dfrac{MS_{subj}}{MS_{error}}$
Error	SS_{error}	df_{error}	$\dfrac{SS_{error}}{df_{error}}$	
Total	SS_{tot}	df_{tot}		

The error variance represents individual differences between subjects *within* each of the conditions due to irrelevant variables affecting the performance of subjects. It is this error variance which is compared with the between conditions variance in the F ratio.

The general method for calculating the sums of squares for each source of variance is exactly the same as that used for the unrelated ANOVA design, except that we have to calculate an additional sum of squares for 'subjects'. We shall again be calculating each SS by summing together squared scores and subtracting the same *constant*, the grand total of scores squared divided by the total number of scores in the table. The N in this case refers to all eighteen scores taken from the six subjects.

For SS_{bet} we need to add the squares of the totals for the experimental conditions in order to calculate the predicted variance in subjects' scores as a result of differences between conditions.

For SS_{subj} we add up the squares of the totals for each subject across all three conditions in order to calculate the variance due to individuals' overall performance.

For SS_{tot} we add up the squares of all the individual scores since these represent the total variability in subjects' scores.

The SS_{error} represents all the variability in scores 'left over' after the variability due to experimental conditions (SS_{bet}) and to different subjects' performance (SS_{subj}) have been subtracted from the total variance (SS_{tot}).

The degrees of freedom (df) are calculated in a similar way. The df for SS_{bet} are the number of conditions minus one. The df for SS_{subj} are the number of subjects minus one. The df for SS_{tot} are the total number of scores minus one. And the df for SS_{error} are obtained by subtracting the df_{bet} and the df_{subj} from the total df (see Progress Box Twelve).

The F ratio for between conditions represents the size of the variance due to experimental conditions in relation to error variance. To be significant the observed value of the statistic F has to be *equal* to or *larger* than the critical values in Table I.

Step-by-Step Instructions for Calculating the Value of F

Calculate SS from the following formulae (using the scores in Table 27) where

$\sum T_c^2$ = sum of the squared totals for each condition $\qquad$ $\sum T_c^2 = 43^2 + 37^2 + 24^2$

$\sum T_s^2$ = sum of the squared totals for each subject $\qquad$ $\sum T_s^2 = 19^2 + 20^2 + 17^2 + 15^2 + 14^2 + 19^2$

n = number of subjects $\qquad$ $n = 6$

c = number of scores for each subject (i.e. number of conditions) $\qquad$ $c = 3$

N = total number of scores $\qquad$ $N = 18$

$(\sum x)^2$ = grand total squared $\qquad$ $(\sum x)^2 = 104^2$

$\dfrac{(\sum x)^2}{N}$ = *constant* to be subtracted from all SS

x = each individual score

$\sum x^2$ = sum of squared individual scores

Note the difference between $\sum x^2$ when individual scores are first squared and then added and $(\sum x)^2$ when individual scores are first added up to make a grand total, which is then squared.

1 Calculate SS_{bet} from the formula

$$\frac{\sum T_c^2}{n} - \frac{(\sum x)^2}{N} \qquad SS_{bet} = \frac{43^2 + 37^2 + 24^2}{6} - \frac{104^2}{18}$$

$$= \frac{3794}{6} - \frac{10816}{18}$$

$$= 632.33 - 600.89$$

$$= 31.44$$

2 Calculate SS_{subj} from the formula

$$\frac{\sum T_s^2}{c} - \frac{(\sum x)^2}{N}$$

$$SS_{subj} = \frac{19^2 + 20^2 + 17^2 + 15^2 + 14^2 + 19^2}{3} - \frac{104^2}{18}$$

$$= \frac{1832}{3} - \frac{10816}{18}$$

$$= 610.67 - 600.89$$

$$= 9.78$$

3 Calculate SS_{tot} from the formula

$$\sum x^2 - \frac{(\sum x)^2}{N}$$

$$SS_{tot} = 8^2 + 7^2 + 9^2 + 5^2 + 6^2$$
$$+ 8^2 + 7^2 + 8^2 + 5^2 + 4^2$$
$$+ 6^2 + 7^2 + 4^2 + 5^2 + 3^2$$
$$+ 6^2 + 2^2 + 4^2 - \frac{104^2}{18}$$

$$= 664 - \frac{10816}{18}$$

$$= 664 - 600.89$$

$$= 63.11$$

4 Calculate SS_{error} from the formula
$SS_{tot} - SS_{bet} - SS_{subj}$

$$SS_{error} = 63.11 - 31.44 - 9.78$$
$$= 21.89$$

5 Calculate the degrees of freedom

df_{bet} = number of conditions $- 1$

df_{subj} = number of subjects $- 1$

$df_{tot} = N - 1$

$df_{error} = df_{tot} - df_{bet} - df_{subj}$

$df_{bet} = 3 - 1 = 2$

$df_{subj} = 6 - 1 = 5$

$df_{tot} = 18 - 1 = 17$

$df_{error} = 17 - 2 - 5 = 10$

6 Divide each SS by df to obtain MS

$$MS_{bet} = \frac{SS_{bet}}{df_{bet}}$$

$$MS_{subj} = \frac{SS_{subj}}{df_{subj}}$$

$$MS_{error} = \frac{SS_{error}}{df_{error}}$$

$$MS_{bet} = \frac{31.44}{2} = 15.72$$

$$MS_{subj} = \frac{9.78}{5} = 1.956$$

$$MS_{error} = \frac{21.89}{10} = 2.189$$

7   Calculate F ratios for MS_{bet} over MS_{error} and for MS_{subj} over MS_{error}, allocating the correct df to the F ratios

$$F \text{ ratio for } MS_{bet} = \frac{MS_{bet}}{MS_{error}} \qquad F_{2,10} = \frac{15.72}{2.189} = 7.18$$

$$F \text{ ratio for } MS_{subj} = \frac{MS_{subj}}{MS_{error}} \qquad F_{5,10} = \frac{1.956}{2.189} = .8935$$

8   Complete the ANOVA table in Table 29

Table 29   ANOVA table

Source of variance	Sums of squares (SS)	Degrees of freedom (df)	Mean squares (MS)	F ratios
Presentation rate variable	31.44	2	15.72	$F_{2,10} = 7.18$
Subjects	9.78	5	1.956	$F_{5,10} = .8935$
Error	21.89	10	2.189	
Total	63.11	17		

Looking up Significance in Tables I(1)–(4)

Starting with Table I(1) we locate the degrees of freedom for between conditions (df_{bet}) along the v_1 row and the degrees of freedom for the error (df_{error}) down the v_2 column. Where they intersect is the critical value of F for these df. In our example, for between conditions, $v_1 = 2$, $v_2 = 10$, the critical value is 4.10. Since our observed F value of 7.18 for between conditions is larger than this, we can reject the null hypothesis and conclude that there is a significant effect of presentation rate on recall $(p < .05)$. For subjects, $v_1 = 5$, $v_2 = 10$, the critical value is 3.33. The observed F value of .8935 for subjects is less and therefore the overall differences between subjects are not significant.

If you look at Tables I(2)–(4), you will see that our observed $F_{2,10}$ for between conditions of 7.18 is larger than the critical value of 5.46 in Table I(2) but not in Table I(3). So the predicted effects of presentation rate are significant at $p < .025$ but not at $p < .01$. As with the unrelated ANOVA you may wish to use a trend test to test whether there is a trend in scores (in this case Page's L trend test—see Chapter 6, Section 6.4).

Question 27

Subject	Variable A		Total
	A_1	A_2	
1	3	2	5
2	6	4	10
3	4	3	7
4	9	3	12
5	5	4	9
Total	27	16	43

(a) Analyse the above data using a one-way *related* ANOVA design. Follow the step-by-step instructions for calculating the formulae and filling in an ANOVA table.

(b) Are the results significant? If so, at what level of significance?

8.6 TWO-WAY ANOVA (UNRELATED)

When to Use

This analysis is used when *two* variables are tested with *two or more* conditions for each variable and *different* subjects are used for each of the conditions.

Example

Sixteen different subjects are allocated to four experimental conditions. The four conditions represent two conditions for each of two variables: word length and rate of presentation.

Each subject is presented with a list of ten words. Four subjects are given a list of short words presented at a fast rate; four subjects are given a list of short words presented at a slow rate; four subjects are given a list of long words presented at a fast rate; and four subjects are given a list of long words presented at a slow rate. We predict that there will be a significant interaction between the two variables, with more short words being recalled at a fast rate of presentation but more long words at a slow presentation rate. The results are presented in a 2 × 2 table as shown in Table 30 (over page).

Notice that there is *one* score from each of the four subjects in each condition; also that there are *equal* numbers of subjects in each condition, a necessary assumption for all the formulae given below. We have added up the totals for each condition (30, 15, 15, 25), the totals for the two conditions for variable A (45, 40) and for variable B (which also happen to be 45, 40) and the grand total (85).

Table 30   Table of results

Variable B (rate of presentation)	Variable A (word length)		Totals B (T_b)
	A_1 (short words)	A_2 (long words)	
B_1 (fast rate)	9 8 6 7	5 3 3 4	
	30	15	45
B_2 (slow rate)	4 3 3 5	7 5 6 7	
	15	25	40
Totals A (T_a)			Grand total
	45	40	85

Sources of Variance Table

For a 2 × 2 *unrelated* design the sources of variance table is more complicated than for one-way ANOVA (Table 31). This is because we are dealing with *two* variables and the interaction between them.

Table 31   Sources of variance table for 2 × 2 unrelated design

Source of variance	Sums of squares (SS)	Degrees of freedom (df)	Mean squares (MS)	F ratios
Variable A (word length)	SS_A	df_A	$\dfrac{SS_A}{df_A}$	$\dfrac{MS_A}{MS_{error}}$
Variable B (presentation rate)	SS_B	df_B	$\dfrac{SS_B}{df_B}$	$\dfrac{MS_B}{MS_{error}}$
A × B (interaction)	SS_{AB}	df_{AB}	$\dfrac{SS_{AB}}{df_{AB}}$	$\dfrac{MS_{AB}}{MS_{error}}$
Error	SS_{error}	df_{error}	$\dfrac{SS_{error}}{df_{error}}$	
Total	SS_{tot}	df_{tot}		

Rationale

You will notice that with this design we have two variables, A and B, each of which has two conditions, plus the interaction between them. All these are predicted differences *between conditions*. If you look back to the one-way unrelated ANOVA table in section 8.4, what this amounts to is that the SS_{bet} variance has been divided into three parts, i.e. the A, B and $A \times B$ variances.

As with the unrelated one-way ANOVA, these differences between conditions are also differences between the different groups of subjects doing each condition. However, any differences between subjects *within* each condition must be due to irrelevant variables not connected with the predicted differences between conditions, and so constitute the error variance.

As with the one-way ANOVA we calculate sums of squares (SS) for each source of variance, in each case subtracting the same *constant*. Because the SS_{bet} has been apportioned between the A, B and $A \times B$ variance we have to calculate these SS separately.

For SS_A we add up the squares of the totals for the conditions for variable A in order to calculate the predicted variance in subjects' scores due to variable A.

For SS_B we add up the squares of the totals for the variable B conditions for the same reason.

If you look back to the formulae for the one-way ANOVA you will notice that when we were calculating SS_{bet} we divided the squared totals for conditions by n, i.e. the number of subjects doing each condition. With SS_A and SS_B we have to do exactly the same thing. But in this case, looking at Table 30, we see that for SS_A we have to take into account the fact that both the B_1 and the B_2 subjects performed under A_1 (short words) and A_2 (long words). So we need to divide the squared totals for A_1 and A_2 by $n \times b$, i.e. the number of subjects in each condition times the number of B conditions (4×2), which gives the total number of subjects doing each of the A conditions. Similarly, for SS_B we have to divide the squared totals for B_1 and B_2 by $n \times a$, i.e. the number of subjects times the number of A conditions (4×2), which gives the number of subjects doing each of the B conditions.

The easiest way to calculate the $A \times B$ interaction is as follows. Remember that we said that $SS_A + SS_B + SS_{AB}$ all add up to the SS_{bet} in the one-way unrelated ANOVA. So what we do is to calculate the *whole* SS_{bet}, then subtract SS_A and SS_B, thus giving the SS_{AB}. In order to calculate the whole of SS_{bet} we square and sum the totals for all four conditions, i.e. the totals for the four individual 'cells' in Table 30 which represent the individual experimental conditions for all the combinations of the A and B variables (i.e. 30, 15, 15, 25). The notation for this is $\sum T_{ab}^2$ to show that we are adding up each of the a/b group combinations. This time we need to divide by the number of subjects in each condition, giving for SS_{bet} the formula $\dfrac{\sum T_{ab}^2}{n} - \dfrac{(\sum x)^2}{N}$.

To obtain the $A \times B$ interaction we subtract SS_A and SS_B from the whole SS_{bet} to give the interaction SS_{AB}.

For SS_{tot} as usual we add up the squares of all the individual scores since these represent the total variability in subjects' scores.

The SS_{error} reflects all the variability in scores 'left over' after the variance due to variables and interactions have been subtracted from total variance. So $SS_{error} = SS_{tot} - SS_A - SS_B - SS_{AB}$.

The degrees of freedom (df) are calculated in a similar way. The df for SS_A are the number of conditions for variable A minus one. The df SS_B are the number of conditions for variable B minus one. The df for SS_{AB} are the df for SS_A multiplied by the df for SS_B. The df for SS_{tot} are the total number of scores minus one. And the df for SS_{error} are obtained by subtracting all the other df from the total df (see Progress Box Twelve).

The F ratios for A, B and $A \times B$ represent the size of the variances due to variable A, variable B and the $A \times B$ interaction between the variables in relation to error variance. To be significant the observed value of the statistic F has to be *equal* to or *larger* than the critical values in Table I.

Step-by-Step Instructions for Calculating the value of F

Calculate SS from the following formulae (using the scores in Table 30) where

$\sum T_a^2$ = sum of squared totals for $\sum T_a^2 = 45^2 + 40^2$
       A conditions

$\sum T_b^2$ = sum of squared totals for $\sum T_b^2 = 45^2 + 40^2$
       B conditions

$\sum T_{ab}^2$ = the sum of squared totals for $\sum T_{ab}^2 = 30^2 + 15^2 + 15^2 + 25^2$
       combined AB conditions, i.e. the
       individual 'cells' in Table 30

       n = number of subjects in each $n = 4$
         condition

       a = number of conditions for $a = 2$
         variable A

       b = number of conditions for $b = 2$
         variable B

       N = total number of scores $N = 16$

$(\sum x)^2$ = grand total squared $(\sum x)^2 = 85^2$

$\dfrac{(\sum x)^2}{N}$ = *constant* to be subtracted
       from all SS

$\sum x^2$ = sum of squared individual scores

See instructions for one-way ANOVA for the difference between $\sum x^2$ and $(\sum x)^2$.

1   Calculate SS_A from the formula

$$\frac{\sum T_a^2}{nb} - \frac{(\sum x)^2}{N}$$

$$SS_A = \frac{45^2 + 40^2}{4 \times 2} - \frac{85^2}{16}$$

$$= \frac{3625}{8} - \frac{7225}{16}$$

$$= 453.125 - 451.5625$$

$$= 1.5625$$

2   Calculate SS_B from the formula

$$\frac{\sum T_b^2}{na} - \frac{(\sum x)^2}{N}$$

$$SS_B = \frac{45^2 + 40^2}{4 \times 2} - \frac{85^2}{16}$$

$$= \frac{3625}{8} - \frac{7225}{16}$$

$$= 453.125 - 451.5625$$

$$= 1.5625$$

3   Calculate SS_{AB} from the formula

$$\frac{\sum T_{ab}^2}{n} - \frac{(\sum x)^2}{N} - SS_A - SS_B$$

Note that you have already calculated SS_A and SS_B and the constant

$$SS_{AB} = \frac{30^2 + 15^2 + 15^2 + 25^2}{4}$$

$$- 451.5625$$
$$- 1.5625 - 1.5625$$
$$= 493.75 - 451.5625$$
$$- 1.5625 - 1.5625$$
$$= 39.0625$$

4   Calculate SS_{tot} from the formula

$$\sum x^2 - \frac{(\sum x)^2}{N}$$

$$SS_{tot} = 9^2 + 8^2 + 6^2 + 7^2 + \ldots$$

$$+ 5^2 + 6^2 + 7^2 - \frac{85^2}{16}$$

$$= 507 - 451.5625$$

$$= 55.4375$$

5   Calculate SS_{error} from the formula
     $$SS_{tot} - SS_A - SS_B - SS_{AB}$$

$$SS_{error} = 55.4375 - 1.5625$$
$$- 1.5625 - 39.0625$$

$$= 13.25$$

6   Calculate the degrees of freedom

df_A = number of conditions $df_A = 2 - 1 = 1$
           $A - 1$

df_B = number of conditions $df_B = 2 - 1 = 1$
           $B - 1$

$df_{AB} = df_A \times df_B$ $df_{AB} = 1 \times 1 = 1$

$df_{tot} = N - 1$ $df_{tot} = 16 - 1 = 15$

$df_{error} = df_{tot} - df_A - df_B - df_{AB}$ $df_{error} = 15 - 1 - 1 - 1 = 12$

7   Divide each SS by df to obtain
     MS

$$MS_A = \frac{SS_A}{df_A}$$ $$MS_A = \frac{1.5625}{1} = 1.5625$$

$$MS_B = \frac{SS_B}{df_B}$$ $$MS_B = \frac{1.5625}{1} = 1.5625$$

$$MS_{AB} = \frac{SS_{AB}}{df_{AB}}$$ $$MS_{AB} = \frac{39.0625}{1} = 39.0625$$

$$MS_{error} = \frac{SS_{error}}{df_{error}}$$ $$MS_{error} = \frac{13.25}{12} = 1.104$$

8   Calculate F ratios for MS_A, MS_B
     and MS_{AB}, allocating the correct
     df to the F ratios

F ratio for $MS_A = \dfrac{MS_A}{MS_{error}}$ $F_{1,12} = \dfrac{1.5625}{1.104} = 1.415$

F ratio for $MS_B = \dfrac{MS_B}{MS_{error}}$ $F_{1,12} = \dfrac{1.5625}{1.104} = 1.415$

F ratio for $MS_{AB} = \dfrac{MS_{AB}}{MS_{error}}$ $F_{1,12} = \dfrac{39.0625}{1.104} = 35.38$

9   Complete the ANOVA table in Table 32

Looking up Significance in Tables I(1)–(4)

We have to locate the appropriate df. For all the F ratios in Table 32, $v_1 = 1$
and $v_2 = 12$. The critical value of F in Table I(1) is 4.75. Since the observed
F ratios for variable A and variable B are smaller than this, neither the main
effects of world length nor of presentation rate are significant. However,

the observed F ratio of 35.38 for the interaction $A \times B$ is larger than the critical value in Table I(1), and indeed larger than the critical values for $v_1 = 1, v_2 = 12$ in Tables I(2)–(4), indicating that it is significant at $p < .001$. So it seems that neither the variable of word length nor the variable of rate of presentation alone caused differences in subjects' scores. However, if we look back to the totals for the four separate AB conditions in Table 30, we can see that recall scores for short and long words differed considerably according to whether they were presented at a fast or slow presentation rate. Recall for short words was 30 at a fast rate and only 15 at the slow presentation rate. In contrast, recall for long words was better at the slow rate (25) and worse at the fast rate (15). In other words, the prediction we made about the interaction between the variables has been supported at a high level of significance ($p < .001$).

Table 32   ANOVA table

Source of variance	Sums of squares (SS)	Degrees of freedom (df)	Mean squares (MS)	F ratios
Variable A (word length)	1.5625	1	1.5625	$F_{1,12} = 1.415$
Variable B (presentation rate)	1.5625	1	1.5625	$F_{1,12} = 1.415$
$A \times B$ (interaction)	39.0625	1	39.0625	$F_{1,12} = 35.38$
Error	13.25	12	1.104	
Total	55.4375	15		

Question 28

Variable B	Variable A		
	A_1	A_1	Totals B
B_1	7	2	
	9	1	
	6	2	
	22	5	27
B_2	6	3	
	6	3	
	5	2	
	17	8	25
B_3	3	5	
	1	6	
	1	4	
	5	15	20
Totals A	44	28	72

(a) Try doing a 2×3 *unrelated* ANOVA on the above data, obtained from six groups of three different subjects. You can use the same formulae as in the step-by-step instructions but for variable *B* there will be *three* conditions instead of two. Fill in the appropriate ANOVA table.

(b) Do either of the variables or the interaction have a significant effect on subjects' scores?

8.7 TWO-WAY ANOVA (RELATED)

When to Use

This analysis is used when *two* variables are tested with *two or more* conditions for each variable and the *same* (or *matched*) subjects are used for all experimental conditions.

Example

Four subjects are all tested under four conditions, representing a combination of two levels of variable *A* (word length) and two levels of variable *B* (rate of presentation).

We predict that the rate of presentation and the word length variables will have a significant effect on the dependent variable of recalled scores. Subjects will be able to recall more short words than long words and scores will be significantly higher with a slow rate of presentation. We also predict that there will be no interaction between the two variables A and B. These results are set out in Table 33.

Table 33   Table of results

| Subject | A_1 (short words) | | A_2 (long words) | |
	B_1 (fast rate)	B_2 (slow rate)	B_1 (fast rate)	B_2 (slow rate)
1	7	7	3	5
2	5	6	1	3
3	6	8	2	5
4	4	9	2	4

Sources of Variance Table

As indicated below, the ANOVA table for a 2 × 2 *related* design is complicated by the addition of subjects as a separate source of variance (Table 34).

Table 34   Sources of variable table

Source of variance	Sums of squares (SS)	Degrees of freedom (df)	Mean squares (MS)	F ratios
Variable A (word length)	SS_A	df_A	$\dfrac{SS_A}{df_A}$	$\dfrac{MS_A}{MS_{AS}}$
Variable B (presentation rate)	SS_B	df_B	$\dfrac{SS_B}{df_B}$	$\dfrac{MS_B}{MS_{BS}}$
S (subjects)	SS_S	df_S	$\dfrac{SS_S}{df_S}$	$\dfrac{MS_S}{MS_{ABS}}$
$A \times B$ (interaction)	SS_{AB}	df_{AB}	$\dfrac{SS_{AB}}{df_{AB}}$	$\dfrac{MS_{AB}}{MS_{ABS}}$
Error AS	SS_{AS}	df_{AS}	$\dfrac{SS_{AS}}{df_{AS}}$	
Error BS	SS_{BS}	df_{BS}	$\dfrac{SS_{BS}}{df_{BS}}$	
Error ABS	SS_{ABS}	df_{ABS}	$\dfrac{SS_{ABS}}{df_{ABS}}$	
Total	SS_{tot}	df_{tot}		

Rationale

As with the one-way related ANOVA (Selection 8.5) the overall differences between subjects across conditions can be treated as if they were a separate source of variance. So for a 2×2 related design the sources of variance table has to include not only the two variables A and B but also a third variable, subjects (S). The effect of this extra S variable on the calculations is quite dramatic, because now we have to take into account not only the interaction between the two variables ($A \times B$) but also the appropriate error variances of each of the variables separately, AS, BS and ABS, which represent in each case the individual differences between subjects *within* each of these conditions. You will see, therefore, in Table 34 that the F ratios for A, B and $A \times B$ include different error terms. To sum up, you can think of this design as a 2×2 design (like the two-way unrelated ANOVA shown in Section 8.6) but with a *third* variable of the differences between individual subjects' overall performance across all conditions. This is made possible by the fact that the same subjects are doing all the conditions, whereas in the unrelated two-way each subject was performing under only one of the four conditions.

The general method for calculating the sum of squares for each source of variance is identical to the method detailed in the previous analyses, in that we calculate sums of squares and subtract a *constant*. However, when there are three or more variables, it helps if we separate the scores and rearrange them into three 2×2 tables showing the scores and totals for the AB conditions, the AS conditions and the BS conditions. In effect, this splits the data into one unrelated 2×2 table for the variables A and B (Table 35(a)) and two related tables for A and subjects (Table 35(b)) and B and subjects (Table 35(c)). You will notice that each of the summary tables

Table 35   (a) AB summary table

	A_1		A_2		Totals B (T_b)
B_1	7	5	3	1	
	6	4	2	2	30
	22		8		
B_2	7	6	5	3	
	8	9	5	4	47
	30		17		
Totals A (T_a)	52		25		Grand total 77

(b) *AS* summary table

	A_1		A_2		Totals S (T_s)
6 S_1	7	7	3	5	22
		14		8	
S_2	5	6	1	3	15
		11		4	
S_3	6	8	2	5	21
		14		7	
S_4	4	9	2	4	19
		13		6	
Totals A (T_a)		52		25	Grand total 77

(c) *BS* summary table

	B_1		B_2		Totals S (T_s)
S_1	7	3	7	5	22
		10		12	
S_2	5	1	6	3	15
		6		9	
S_3	6	2	8	5	21
		8		13	
S_4	4	2	9	4	19
		6		13	
Totals B (T_b)		30		47	Grand total 77

You will notice that each of the summary tables contains all the scores for each subject in Table 33 but in different combinations of conditions. You can check that all subjects' scores are included in each summary table by noting that the grand total of all scores is the same for each table.

The basic idea is that SS_A, SS_B and SS_{AB} can be calculated from Table 35(a), which is just like a 2×2 unrelated ANOVA with the variance due to subjects' overall performance left out.

When we come to the SS_S for subjects we can use either Table 35(b) or (c) to add up the squares of the totals for each of the four subjects across all conditions (T_s).

To calculate the interaction S_{AS} we use Table 35(b). We calculate all the variance due to variable A and subjects together and subtract the individual variances for A and S.

For the SS_{BS} interaction you do the same using Table 35(c).

Finally, the general error due to SS_{ABS} is calculated by subtracting all the other SS from the SS_{tot}.

You might also like to note a quick method for deciding what to divide each set of summed squares by. In each case it is the number of conditions or subjects (i.e. a, b or n) which are *not* mentioned in the summed totals ($n = s$ for this purpose because both refer to number of subjects). For example, in the formula for SS_{AS}, $\sum T_{as}^2$ is divided by b, i.e. the two conditions for variable B, because that is the only variable not mentioned in $\sum T_{as}^2$. Similarly, $\sum T_a^2$ is divided by $n \times b$ and $\sum T_s^2$ by $a \times b$. The point is that in each case we are dividing by the number of scores that went to make up these totals.

This all sounds extremely complicated but you will find that it works out quite easily when you follow through the step-by-step instructions.

The degrees of freedom (df) for A, B and $A \times B$ are calculated as you would expect. The df for SS_S are the number of subjects minus one; the df for SS_{AS} are the df for SS_A multiplied by the df for SS_S; the df for SS_{BS} are the df for SS_B multiplied by the df for SS_S; the df for SS_{ABS} are the df for SS_A multiplied by the df for SS_B multiplied by the df for SS_S. The df for SS_{tot} are all the scores minus one. The df for SS_{ABS} could also be obtained by subtracting all the other df from the df for SS_{tot}.

The F ratios for $A, B, A \times B$ represent the size of the variances due to experimental conditions and interactions in relation to error variance. To be significant the observed value of the statistic F has to be *equal* to or *larger* than the critical values in Table I.

Step-by-Step Instructions for Calculating the Value of F

Using Tables 35(a)–(c) calculate SS using the following formulae where

$\sum T_a^2$ = sum of squared totals for A conditions from Table 35(a)

$\sum T_a^2 = 52^2 + 25^2$

$\sum T_b^2$ = sum of squared totals for B conditions from Table 35(a)

$\sum T_b^2 = 30^2 + 47^2$

$\sum T_s^2$ = sum of squared totals for each subject from Table 35(b)

$\sum T_s^2 = 22^2 + 15^2 + 21^2 + 19^2$

$\sum T_{ab}^2$ = sum of squared totals for combined AB conditions, i.e. the individual cells in Table 35(a)

$\sum T_{ab}^2 = 22^2 + 30^2 + 8^2 + 17^2$

$\sum T_{as}^2$ = sum of squared totals for combined $A \times S$ conditions, i.e. the individual cells in Table 35(b)

$\sum T_{as}^2 = 14^2 + 11^2 + 14^2 + 13^2$
$+ 8^2 + 4^2 + 7^2 + 6^2$

$\sum T_{bs}^2$ = sum of squared totals for combined $B \times S$ conditions, i.e. the individual cells in Table 35(c)

$\sum T_{bs}^2 = 10^2 + 6^2 + 8^2 + 6^2$
$+ 12^2 + 9^2 + 13^2 + 13^2$

n = number of subjects

$n = 4$

a = number of conditions for variable A

$a = 2$

b = number of conditions for variable B

$b = 2$

N = total number of scores

$N = 16$

$(\sum x)^2$ = grand total squared

$(\sum x)^2 = 77^2$

$\dfrac{(\sum x)^2}{N}$ = *constant* to be subtracted from all SS

$\sum x^2$ = sum of squared individual scores

1   Calculate SS_A from the formula

$$\frac{\sum T_a^2}{nb} - \frac{(\sum x)^2}{N}$$

$$SS_A = \frac{52^2 + 25^2}{4 \times 2} - \frac{77^2}{16}$$

$$= \frac{3329}{8} - \frac{5929}{16}$$

$$= 416.125 - 370.5625$$

$$= 45.5625$$

2   Calculate SS_B from the formula

$$\frac{\sum T_b^2}{na} - \frac{(\sum x)^2}{N}$$

$$SS_B = \frac{30^2 + 47^2}{4 \times 2} - \frac{77^2}{16}$$

$$= \frac{3109}{8} - 370.5625$$

$$388.625 - 370.5625$$

$$= 18.0625$$

3   Calculate SS_S from the formula

$$\frac{\sum T_s^2}{ab} - \frac{(\sum x)^2}{N}$$

$$SS_S = \frac{22^2 + 15^2 + 21^2 + 19^2}{4}$$

$$- 370.5625$$

$$= \frac{1511}{4} - 370.5625$$

$$= 377.75 - 370.5625$$

$$= 7.1875$$

4   Calculate SS_{AB} from the formula

$$\frac{\sum T_{ab}^2}{n} - \frac{(\sum x)^2}{N} - SS_A - SS_B$$

$$SS_{AB} = \frac{22^2 + 30^2 + 8^2 + 17^2}{4}$$

$$- 370.5625 - 45.5625$$

$$- 18.0625$$

$$= 434.25 - 370.5625$$

$$- 45.5625 - 18.0625$$

$$= .0625$$

5   Calculate SS_{AS} from the formula

$$\frac{\sum T_{as}^2}{b} - \frac{(\sum x)^2}{N} - SS_A - SS_S$$

$$SS_{AS} = \frac{14^2 + 11^2 + 14^2 + 13^2 + 8^2 + 4^2 + 7^2 + 6^2}{2}$$

$$- 370.5625 - 45.5625 - 7.1875$$

$$= 423.5 - 370.5625 - 45.5625 - 7.1875$$

$$= .1875$$

6   Calculate SS_{BS} from the formula

$$\frac{\sum T_{bs}^2}{a} - \frac{(\sum x^2)}{N} - SS_B - SS_S$$

$$SS_{BS} = \frac{10^2 + 6^2 + 8^2 + 6^2 + 12^2 + 9^2 + 13^2 + 13^2}{2}$$

$$- 370.5625 - 18.0625 - 7.1875$$

$$= 399.5 - 370.5625 - 18.0625 - 7.1875$$

$$= 3.6875$$

7   Calculate SS_{tot} from the formula

$$\sum x^2 - \frac{(\sum x)^2}{N}$$

$$SS_{tot} = (7^2 + 5^2 + 6^2 + \dots$$
$$+ 5^2 + 3^2 + 5^2 + 4^2)$$
$$- 370.5625$$
$$= 449 - 370.5625$$
$$= 78.4375$$

8   Calculate SS_{ABS} from the formula

$$SS_{tot} - SS_A - SS_B - SS_S$$
$$- SS_{AB} - SS_{AS} - SS_{BS}$$

$$SS_{ABS} = 78.4375 - 45.5625$$
$$- 18.0625 - 7.1875$$
$$- .0625 - .1875$$
$$- 3.6875$$
$$= 3.6875$$

9   Calculate the degrees of freedom

df_A	= number of conditions $A - 1$	$df_A = 2 - 1 = 1$
df_B	= number of conditions $B - 1$	$df_B = 2 - 1 = 1$
df_S	= number of subjects $n - 1$	$df_S = 4 - 1 = 3$
df_{AB}	$= df_A \times df_B$	$df_{AB} = 1 \times 1 = 1$
df_{AS}	$= df_A \times df_S$	$df_{AS} = 1 \times 3 = 3$
df_{BS}	$= df_B \times df_S$	$df_{BS} = 1 \times 3 = 3$
df_{ABS}	$= df_A \times df_B \times df_S$	$df_{ABS} = 1 \times 1 \times 3 = 3$
df_{tot}	$= N - 1$	$df_{tot} = 16 - 1 = 15$

10   Divide each SS by df to obtain
      MS

$$MS_A = \frac{SS_A}{df_A}$$

$$MS_A = \frac{45.5625}{1} = 45.5625$$

$$MS_B = \frac{SS_B}{df_B}$$

$$MS_B = \frac{18.0625}{1} = 18.0625$$

$$MS_S = \frac{SS_S}{df_S}$$

$$MS_S = \frac{7.1875}{?} = 2.3958$$

$$MS_{AB} = \frac{SS_{AB}}{df_{AB}}$$

$$MS_{AB} = \frac{.0625}{1} = .0625$$

$$MS_{AS} = \frac{SS_{AS}}{df_{AS}}$$

$$MS_{AS} = \frac{.1875}{3} = .0625$$

$$MS_{BS} = \frac{SS_{BS}}{df_{BS}}$$

$$MS_{BS} = \frac{3.6875}{3} = 1.229$$

$$MS_{ABS} = \frac{SS_{ABS}}{df_{ABS}}$$

$$MS_{ABS} = \frac{3.6875}{3} = 1.229$$

11   Calculate F ratios allocating
      correct df

$$F \text{ ratio for } MS_A = \frac{MS_A}{MS_{AS}}$$

$$F_{1,3} = \frac{45.5625}{.0625} = 729$$

$$F \text{ ratio for } MS_B = \frac{MS_B}{MS_{BS}}$$

$$F_{1,3} = \frac{18.0625}{1.229} = 14.697$$

$$F \text{ ratio for } MS_S = \frac{MS_S}{MS_{ABS}}$$

$$F_{3,3} = \frac{2.3958}{1.229} = 1.949$$

$$F \text{ ratio for } MS_{AB} = \frac{MS_{AB}}{MS_{ABS}}$$

$$F_{1,3} = \frac{.0625}{1.229} = .051$$

12   Complete the ANOVA table in
      Table 36

Table 36 ANOVA table

Source of variance	Sums of squares (SS)	Degrees of freedom (df)	Mean squares (MS)	F ratios
Variable A (word length)	45.5625	1	45.5625	$F_{1,3} = 729$
Variable B (presentation rate)	18.0625	1	18.0625	$F_{1,3} = 14.697$
S (subjects)	7.1875	3	2.3958	$F_{3,3} = 1.949$
A × B (interaction)	.0625	1	.0625	$F_{1,3} = .051$
Error AS	.1875	3	.0625	
Error BS	3.6875	3	1.229	
Error ABS	3.6875	3	1.229	
Total	78.4375	15		

Looking up Significance in Tables I(1)–(4)

In Table I(4) the critical value for $F_{1,3}$ is 167.0 at the $p < .001$ level of significance. Since the observed value of F for variable A is 729, the predicted effect of word length on recall scores is significant at this level, i.e. more short words are recalled in Condition A_1.

In Table I(1) the critical value for $F_{1,3}$ is 10.13 at the $p < .05$ level of significance. Since the observed value of F for variable B is 14.697, the effect of presentation rate on recall scores is significant at this level.

The observed value for the interaction $A \times B$ of $F_{1,3} = .051$ is not, however, significant at any of the levels given in Tables I(1)–(4), since it is smaller than any of the critical values.

It is usual also to check the F value for the subjects variance; in this case the observed value of $F_{3,3} = 1.949$ is not significant.

8.8 TWO-WAY ANOVA (MIXED)

When to Use

This analysis is used in the special case when *two* variables are tested with *two or more* conditions but for one of the variables *different* subjects are used for each condition and for the other variable the *same* subjects are used for all the conditions. The reasons why you might want to use same or different subjects for one or other of the variables are discussed in Chapter 2, Section 2.3.

Example

Nine subjects are allocated in groups of three to each of the three conditions for variable *A* (word length). Each of these subjects is tested under *all* three conditions for variable *B* (rate of presentation). In other words, each subject is presented with *three* lists of words: S_1, S_2 and S_3 with short words, S_4, S_5, S_6 with medium length words, S_7, S_8, S_9 with long words. But *all* the subjects are presented with one of his or her lists at a fast rate, one at a medium rate and one at a slow rate. Thus each subject does only *one* of the word length conditions but all *three* of the presentation rates. The order of these presentation rates has, of course, to be counterbalanced to arrive at a different order for each subject.

This design is a two way 3 × 3 design, because it has *two* variables, each with *three* conditions. The word length conditions are done by *different* subjects (i.e. *between* subjects) and the presentation rate conditions are done by the *same* subjects (*within* subjects).

In Table 37 each square represents the scores for the three subjects doing each of the variable *A* conditions under the three variable *B* presentation rates. We also show totals for each of the conditions, for each of the subjects, for each of the variables and the grand total.

Rationale

The general method for calculating sums of squares for each source of variance is the same as for the simpler ANOVAs, squaring the appropriate totals and subtracting a *constant*. As with the two-way related ANOVA, for each variable a different error variance has to be calculated representing the interaction between the variance due to the conditions of that variable and the individual differences between subjects within each of these conditions. The only difference with the mixed case is that, since it is only the variable *B* conditions which are being done by all subjects, it is not possible to calculate a variance due to subjects' overall performance across both variables. So the error variances are different for the two variables as shown in Table 38.

Sources of Variance Table

The ANOVA table for this mixed design is complicated by the fact that for variable *A* between conditions and 'between subjects' are the same because different groups of subjects are doing the three *A* conditions. However, for variable *B* between conditions are 'within subjects' which means that we can calculate differences between the performance of the nine subjects across the three *B* conditions (Table 38).

Table 37 Table of results

		B_1 (fast rate)	B_2 (medium rate)	B_3 (slow rate)	Totals S (T_s)	Totals A (T_a)
A_1 (short words)	S_1	8	4	3	15	
	S_2	7	4	4	15	44
	S_3	7	5	2	14	
		22	13	9		
A_2 (medium length words)	S_4	4	4	3	11	
	S_5	6	7	5	18	47
	S_6	7	5	6	18	
		17	16	14		
A_3 (long words)	S_7	2	4	6	12	
	S_8	4	6	7	17	43
	S_9	3	6	5	14	
		9	16	18		
					Grand total 134	Grand total 134
Totals B (T_b)		48	45	41		

Table 38 Sources of variance table

Source of variance	Sums of squares (SS)	Degrees of freedom (df)	Mean squares (MS)	F ratios
Variable A (word length)	SS_A	df_A	$\dfrac{SS_A}{df_A}$	$\dfrac{MS_A}{MS_{AS}}$
Error AS	SS_{AS}	df_{AS}	$\dfrac{SS_{AS}}{df_{AS}}$	
Variable B (presentation rate)	SS_B	df_B	$\dfrac{SS_B}{df_B}$	$\dfrac{MS_B}{MS_{B \times AS}}$
$A \times B$ (interaction	SS_{AB}	df_{AB}	$\dfrac{SS_{AB}}{df_{AB}}$	$\dfrac{MS_{AB}}{MS_{B \times AS}}$
Error $B \times AS$	$SS_{B \times AS}$	$df_{B \times AS}$	$\dfrac{SS_{B \times AS}}{df_{B \times AS}}$	
Total	SS_{tot}	df_{tot}		

The degrees of freedom (df) are calculated in the usual way. For A and B the df are the number of conditions minus one and these are multiplied together for $A \times B$. The df for AS is calculated by multiplying the df for subjects, i.e. the number of subjects in each group for variable A minus one, by the number of conditions for variable A. For $B \times AS$ the df can either be obtained by multiplying the *df* for *B* and *AS* or by subtracting all the other *df* from the total *df*, i.e. total number of scores minus one.

The *F* ratios for *A, B, A* × *B* represent the size of the variance due to experimental conditions and interactions in relation to error variance. To be significant the observed value of the statistic *F* has to be *equal* to or *larger* than the critical values in Table I.

Step-by-Step Instructions for Calculating the Value of *F*.

Calculate *SS* from the following formulae (using the scores in Table 37 and looking up the various terms in the instructions for the two-way ANOVA (related) in Section 8.7. Note that *n* = number of subjects for each *A* condition).

1   Calculate SS_A from the formula

$$\frac{\sum T_a^2}{nb} - \frac{(\sum x)^2}{N}$$

$$SS_A = \frac{44^2 + 47^2 + 43^2}{3 \times 3} - \frac{134^2}{27}$$

$$= \frac{5994}{9} - \frac{17\,956}{27}$$

$$= 666 - 665.03$$

$$= .97$$

2   Calculate SS_{AS} from the formula

$$\frac{\sum T_s^2}{b} - \frac{(\sum x)^2}{N} - SS_A$$

$$SS_{AS} = \frac{15^2 + 15^2 + 14^2 + 11^2 + 18^2 + 18^2 + 12^2 + 17^2 + 14^2}{3}$$

$$- 665.03 - .97$$

$$= 681.33 - 665.03 - .97$$

$$= 15.33$$

3   Calculate SS_B from the formula

$$\frac{\sum T_b^2}{na} - \frac{(\sum x)^2}{N}$$

$$SS_B = \frac{48^2 + 45^2 + 41^2}{3 \times 3} - 665.03$$

$$= \frac{6010}{9} - 665.03$$

$$= 667.78 - 665.03$$

$$= 2.75$$

4 Calculate SS_{AB} from the formula

$$\frac{\sum T_{ab}^2}{n} - \frac{(\sum x)^2}{N} - SS_A - SS_B$$

$$SS_{AB} = \frac{22^2 + 13^2 + 9^2 + 17^2 + 16^2 + 14^2 + 9^2 + 16^2 + 18^2}{3}$$

$$- 665.03 - .97 - 2.75$$
$$= 712 - 665.03 - .97 - 2.75$$
$$= 43.25$$

5 Calculate SS_{tot} from the formula

$$\sum x^2 - \frac{(\sum x)^2}{N}$$

$$SS_{tot} = 8^2 + 7^2 + 7^2 + \ldots$$
$$+ 6^2 + 7^2 + 5^2 - 665.03$$
$$= 736 - 665.03$$
$$= 70.97$$

6 Calculate $SS_{B \times AS}$ from the formula

$$SS_{tot} - SS_A - SS_{AS} - SS_B - SS_{AB}$$

$$SS_{B \times AS} = 70.97 - .97 - 15.33 - 2.75 - 43.25$$
$$= 8.67$$

7 Calculate the degrees of freedom

df_A = number of conditions $A - 1$ $df_A = 3 - 1 = 2$

df_B = number of conditions $B - 1$ $df_B = 3 - 1 = 2$

$df_{AB} = df_A \times df_B$ $df_{AB} = 2 \times 2 = 4$

df_{AS} = number of subjects in each A condition minus $1 \times$ number of conditions for A $df_{AS} = 2 \times 3 = 6$

$df_{B \times AS} = df_B \times df_{AS}$ $df_{B \times AS} = 2 \times 6 = 12$

$df_{tot} = N - 1$ $df_{tot} = 27 - 1 = 26$

8   Divide each SS by the df to
    obtain MS

$$MS_A = \frac{SS_A}{df_A} \qquad\qquad MS_A = \frac{.97}{2} = .485$$

$$MS_B = \frac{SS_B}{df_B} \qquad\qquad MS_B = \frac{2.75}{2} = 1.375$$

$$MS_{AB} = \frac{SS_{AB}}{df_{AB}} \qquad\qquad MS_{AB} = \frac{43.25}{4} = 10.8125$$

$$MS_{AS} = \frac{SS_{AS}}{df_{AS}} \qquad\qquad MS_{AS} = \frac{15.33}{6} = 2.555$$

$$MS_{B \times AS} = \frac{SS_{B \times AS}}{df_{B \times AS}} \qquad\qquad MS_{B \times AS} = \frac{8.67}{12} = .7225$$

9   Calculate F ratios allocating
    correct df

$$\text{F ratio for } MS_A = \frac{MS_A}{MS_{AS}} \qquad F_{2,6} = \frac{.485}{2.555} = .189$$

$$\text{F ratio for } MS_B = \frac{MS_B}{MS_{B \times AS}} \qquad F_{2,12} = \frac{1.375}{.7225} = 1.903$$

$$\text{F ratio for } MS_{AB} = \frac{MS_{AB}}{MS_{B \times AS}} \qquad F_{4,12} = \frac{10.8125}{.7225} = 14.965$$

10 Complete the ANOVA table in
    Table 39

Table 39   ANOVA table

Source of variance	Sums of squares (SS)	Degrees of freedom (df)	Mean squares (MS)	F ratios
Variable A (word length)	.97	2	.485	$F_{2,6} = .189$
Error AS	15.33	6	2.555	
Variable B (presentation rate)	2.75	2	1.375	$F_{2,12} = 1.903$
$A \times B$ (interaction)	43.25	4	10.8125	$F_{4,12} = 14.965$
Error $B \times AS$	8.67	12	.7225	
Total	70.97	26		

Looking up Significance in Table I(1)–(4)

With $df_{2,6}$ the F ratio for variable A is not significant at any level. Nor is variable B, since the observed F of 1.903 is smaller than the critical value of 3.89 for $F_{2,12}$ in Table I(1). However, the observed F value of 14.965 for the $A \times B$ interaction is larger than the critical value for $F_{4,12}$ of 9.63 in Table I(4) and so is significant at $p < .001$. If you look at the scores for individual conditions in Table 37, you will see that more short words are recalled at the faster rates of presentation but more long words at the slower rates. Medium words have an intermediate amount of recall at every presentation rate.

8.9 EXTENSIONS OF ANOVA

As you have probably realized by now, it is possible to extend the general method for measuring variance by calculating sums of squares and mean squares to an indefinite number of variables and experimental conditions. There is nothing to stop you having five variables, some with two conditions some with three or more, and using same subjects for some variables and different subjects for other variables. The principles are exactly the same as those given in this chapter for working out which totals to add up and the appropriate degrees of freedom.

It is important to display the scores for experimental conditions in a table which shows clearly all the different variables. The example given in Table 40 shows an appropriate layout for an experiment with three variables: variable A with three conditions and variables B and C with two conditions each. Imagine that variable A represents lists of short words (A_1), medium words (A_2) and long words (A_3); variable B fast presentation (B_1) and slow presentation (B_2) rates; and variable C whether subjects were asked to recall the lists after 2 min (C_1) or 30 min (C_2). The scores in the first column in Table 40 would come from those subjects who had to learn a list of short words (A_1) at a fast presentation rate (B_1) and recall the words after 2 min (C_1)— and so on for the other conditions.

You will find some of these more complex designs in advanced statistics textbooks, e.g. Edwards (1968) and Winer (1962). As long as you have made the effort to work through the examples and questions in this chapter, you should find no trouble in following the ANOVA tables and formulae for large-scale experimental designs.

Table 40   ANOVA table for three variables

A_1				A_2				A_3			
B_1		B_2		B_1		B_2		B_1		B_2	
C_1	C_2	C_1	C_2	C_1	C_2	C_1	C_2	C_1	C_2	C_1	C_2

CHAPTER 9

Tests for Correlational Designs

Before we start on correlational statistics, you should turn back to Chapter 1 and read Section 1.3. This introduced the notion of correlational designs and contrasted them with experimental designs which predict differences between experimental conditions. In some research, such as investigating a possible link between smoking and lung cancer, it is unethical to manipulate either variable. In other cases, it may be possible to select groups who represent one variable, like poor and good spellers, and to manipulate the other variable, for example, by exposing them to different reading schemes.

Even with an example of the latter type, a researcher might be interested not so much in the performance of two pre-selected groups, but rather in seeing how the whole range of scores on one variable, e.g. reading scores, maps on to the whole range of scores on another variable, e.g. arithmetic scores. In order to test this, a researcher would measure scores on the two variables by a single group of people, the aim being to investigate the extent to which each individual's performance on each variable correlates with his or her performance on the other variable.

Suppose you have measured both the arithmetic abilities and the reading abilities of a group of twelve children by giving them arithmetic and reading tests and got the results shown in Table 41. What you want to know is whether the child who got the highest arithmetic score also got the highest reading score, whether the child with the next best arithmetic score also got the next best reading score, and so on, down to the child with the worst arithmetic score and the worst reading score. The question at issue is whether reading ability and being good at arithmetic 'go' together or whether there is no connection between the two kinds of ability.

One possible source of confusion may be the relationship between this kind of correlational design and the *same subject* and *different subject* designs we were using in earlier chapters. Obviously, if you want to investigate whether two kinds of performance are found together in the same people, you will always need to compare the performance of the *same* subjects on different tasks.

But how does this differ from experiments in which the same subjects do two experimental conditions and a *difference* is predicted between their performance under the two conditions? In fact, there is *no* difference in the experimental set up. The question is whether the researcher is interested in *differences* between the two conditions or in whether subjects' performance under the two conditions is *correlated*.

Suppose that a researcher was interested in whether a class of twelve children were better at reading or arithmetic. She might give the children standardized arithmetic and reading tests and measure the differences between their scores in the two conditions, i.e. arithmetic test versus reading test.

Table 41   Arithmetic and reading scores

Child	Arithmetic score	Reading score
1	9	2
2	10	3
3	12	1
4	6	1
5	11	4
6	9	1
7	12	5
8	16	8
9	13	5
10	10	3
11	13	6
12	14	7

Question 29

Assume that in Table 41 the arithmetic scores are scored from 1 to 20 and the reading scores from 1 to 10, so that all the reading scores should be doubled to make them comparable. Allowing for this, calculate the means for each condition. Were the children better or worse at arithmetic or reading?

But let us suppose instead that the purpose of the research was to investigate whether there is any relationship between the ability to read and to do arithmetic. In this case the researcher would not be interested in comparing differences between performance on the two tests. As we said earlier, the aim would be to test whether children with high or low scores on one variable also obtained high or low scores on the other variable.

9.1   MEASURING CORRELATIONS

How might you set about investigating whether the two variables of arithmetic ability and reading ability are correlated, high arithmetic and high reading scores tending to go together and low arithmetic and low reading scores tending to go together? Because the same people's scores on both variables are being compared, it is possible to plot these against each other on a graph. To do this you put the possible scores on one test along the horizontal axis and the possible scores on the other test up the vertical

axis (assuming that the possible range of scores for the arithmetic test is
1 to 20 and for the reading test 1 to 10—as shown in Figure 4).

For each child you can fill in a dot to represent its score on both variables.
For instance, the first child in Table 41 would be placed at the spot which
corresponds to a score of 9 on the arithmetic test and a score of 2 on the
reading test. Figure 4 is the graph for all the children in Table 41. Such a
graph is known as a *scattergram* because the scores are 'scattered', each dot
representing the scores on the two tests for each person.

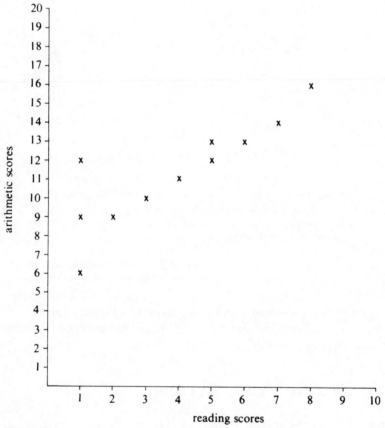

Figure 4

*Check for yourself that these dots represent the scores for the twelve children
in Table 41. Note that child 2 and child 10 had exactly the same scores so they
are represented by the same dot.*

On the basis of the above scores you can see that there is a tendency for children who scored high on the arithmetic test also to have high reading scores, children with medium scores on one measure to have medium scores on the other and children who scored low on one to have low scores on the other. This is shown by the *upward* slope of the dots in Figure 4. Because high scores tend to go together and low scores tend to go together, this is known as a *positive* correlation.

However, there are times when the opposite happens: high scores on one test tend to be associated with low scores on the other test. Suppose that children who are good at arithmetic tend to be slow at reading, while children who score high on reading tend to lag behind in arithmetic. If this were the case, the following test scores for the children might be obtained (Table 42).

Table 42   Arithmetic and reading scores

Child	Arithmetic score	Reading score
1	9	9
2	10	7
3	8	8
4	6	10
5	11	7
6	9	6
7	12	3
8	12	4
9	13	6
10	11	6
11	13	3
12	14	1

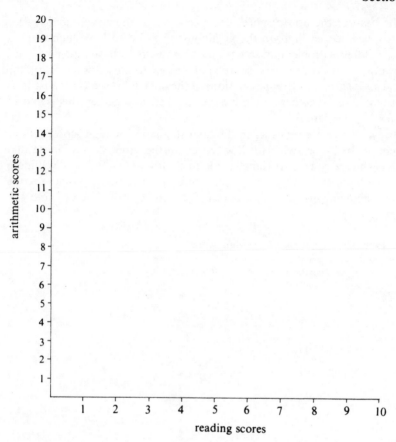

reading scores

Question 30

Plot the scores in Table 42 on the graph. What kind of slope do you get and what do you think it indicates about the relationship between the two sets of scores?

A tendency for high scores on arithmetic to go with low scores on reading and high scores on reading to go with low scores on arithmetic is shown by the *downward* slope of the dots. This is known as a *negative* correlation because it points to a relationship which is the inverse of a positive correlation where high/high and low/low go together.

9.2 TESTING THE SIGNIFICANCE OF CORRELATIONS

If you look at the scattergram in Figure 4 you will see that there is not a completely positive correlation between arithmetic and reading scores. One child who got only 1 on the reading test managed to get the quite high score of 12 for arithmetic. In fact, it would be most unusual to find a perfect one-to-one correlation between scores on two variables. What an experimenter wants to know is whether the amount of correlation he has found is a *significant* relationship.

As with the statistical tests in Chapters 6 and 8, what a correlational significance test tells you is the percentage probability that the scores in your experiment are due to chance fluctuations, as stated by the null hypothesis. Such a scattergram would be one in which the dots are scattered so that there is no particular relationship between the scores on the two variables. On the basis of the percentage probability of a chance result, you can decide whether this probability is sufficiently low to reject the null hypothesis at $p < .05$ or $p < .01$, and instead to accept that there is a significant correlation in the predicted direction.

Incidentally, it is possible to make either a one-tailed or a two-tailed hypothesis about a correlation. A one-tailed hypothesis predicts a correlation in one direction, that is, either a positive correlation is predicted, or a negative correlation is predicted. A two-tailed hypothesis predicts that there will be some correlation between two variables but that it might go in either direction, e.g. that reading scores are likely to be associated either with high or with low arithmetic scores (see Chapter 4, Section 4.3.2).

Correlations are measured in terms of a number from 0 to 1. The scale runs from $+1$ for a perfect positive correlation (all high/high scores together and all low/low scores together) through 0 (no correlation) down to -1 for a perfect negative correlation (all high scores on one variable going with all low scores on the other variable). The nearer a correlation is to 1 or -1 the higher it is. So, for instance, a correlation of .7 indicates a higher correlation between two variables than a correlation of .3.

When you carry out a statistical analysis of correlational data you will end up with a figure between 0 and 1 which expresses the amount of correlation in your data, say, .6. You can then look this correlation up in a statistical table to discover the probability of getting this amount of correlation by chance. So an experimenter might report a correlation of .6 between two variables at a significance level of $p < .05$, meaning that there is a less than 5% probability that it was due to a chance distribution of scores.

Question 31
Which of the following represents the greatest amount of correlation: $+.5, 0, -.65$?

As with other experimental designs, it is possible to use either a non-parametric test (Spearman) or a parametric test (Pearson) to test the significance of a correlational relationship between two variables. Exactly the same considerations apply concerning the criteria which have to be met before using a parametric test as are detailed in Chapter 7, Sections 7.4 and 7.5 and summarized in Progress Box Ten and Progress Box Eleven.

PROGRESS BOX FOURTEEN

1 Correlations represent the degree of association between scores on two variables.

2 Correlations are measured on a scale running from $+1$ (perfect one-to-one *positive* correlation) through 0 (no correlation) down to -1 (perfect one-to-one *negative* correlation).

3 The nearer the size of a correlation is to one ($+1$ or -1) the higher the association between two variables.

4 Statistical tables give percentage probabilities of obtaining correlations of different sizes on a chance basis as predicted by the null hypothesis. For this purpose, positive and negative correlations are treated identically, ignoring the plus or minus sign.

5 Having looked up the percentage probability of obtaining an observed size of correlation, you can decide whether the probability of a chance result is low enough ($p < .05$ or $p < .01$) for you to reject the null hypothesis and accept that there is a significant correlation as predicted by the experimental hypothesis.

9.3 SPEARMAN RANK CORRELATION COEFFICIENT

When to Use

This is a non-parametric test which measures the amount and significance of a *correlation* between people's scores on *two* variables. It should be used when experimental data are measured on an *ordinal* scale or when the data does not meet the other assumptions for parametric tests (see Chapter 7, Section 7.4).

Example

Suppose we are interested in finding out whether there is a relationship between schoolchildren's participation in outdoor games (rated on a ten-point scale from 1 (never plays) to 10 (always joins in)) and the frequency with which children catch colds (rated on a five-point scale from 1 (very frequent) to 5 (very few)). Twelve children were rated on both these scales (normally, of course, a much larger sample of children would be studied). The prediction is that high participation in games will be correlated with a *low* frequency of colds (which you should note is measured as a *high* rating—very few colds—on the five point scale) (see Table 43).

Table 43 Ratings of schoolchildren's participation in outdoor games and frequency of colds

Subject	Variable A (outdoor games rating score) (1–10)	Variable B (number of colds rating score) (1–5)	Rank A	Rank B	d (Rank A – Rank B)	d^2
1	5	2	5	3.5	+ 1.5	2.25
2	3	2	2.5	3.5	– 1	1
3	7	4	7	7.5	– .5	.25
4	10	5	11.5	11	+ .5	.25
5	9	4	9.5	7.5	+ 2	4
6	9	5	9.5	11	– 1.5	2.25
7	2	4	1	7.5	– 6.5	42.25
8	6	3	6	5	+ 1	1
9	3	1	2.5	1.5	+ 1	1
10	4	1	4	1.5	+ 2.5	6.25
11	8	4	8	7.5	+ .5	.25
12	10	5	11.5	11	+ .5	.25

$$\sum d^2 = 61$$

Rationale

If two variables are predicted to be positively correlated, people who have low ratings on one of them should also have low ratings on the other and people who are rated highly on one should also be rated highly on the other. If the ratings on both variables are ranked separately, high ranks on one variable should correspond to high ranks on the other and low ranks on one variable to low ranks on the other. However, if there is no correlation (i.e. a chance distribution of scores as stated by the null hypothesis) the ranks will all be mixed up since a person could have a high rank on one measure and a low rank on the other. The Spearman test calculates the differences between the ranks for the two sets of scores. In order to calculate the statistic called rho (r_s) these differences are subtracted from 1. Obviously the *smaller* the differences between the ranks for the two conditions, the *larger* rho will be, i.e. the nearer to a value of + 1. In the case of a negative correlation, when high ranks on one variable are predicted to be correlated with low ranks on the other, the differences will be large, so that when subtracted from 1 they result in a high negative rho up to a maximum of – 1. To be significant the observed value of rho (r_s) should be *equal* to or *larger* than the critical values in Table J.

Step-by-Step Instructions for Calculating the Value of r_s

1 Rank the scores on variable A, giving 1 to the smallest score and so on (see Chapter 5, Section 5.2). Do the same for the variable B scores

   See Rank A and Rank B columns in Table 43

2 Calculate the difference (d) between each pair of A and B ranks

   See d (Rank A − Rank B) column in Table 43

3 Square each difference between ranks A and B

   See d^2 column in Table 43

4 Add them up to obtain $\sum d^2$

   $\sum d^2 = 61$

5 Count the number of subjects (N)

   $N = 12$

6 Find the value of r_s from the formula

$$r_s = 1 - \frac{6\sum d^2}{N(N^2 - 1)}$$

$$r_s = 1 - \frac{6 \times 61}{12(144 - 1)}$$

$$= 1 - \frac{366}{12 \times 143}$$

$$= 1 - \frac{366}{1716}$$

$$= 1 - .21$$

$$= .79$$

Looking up Significance of rho (r_s) in Table J

Along the top row of the table you will find various levels of significance for one-tailed and two-tailed tests. In the left-hand column you will find the values of N (number of subjects); in our example $N = 12$. The observed r_s value of .79 exceeds the critical value of .777 for $p < .005$ (one-tailed) and you can therefore conclude that there is a significant relationship between the two variables. (Note that some values of N (number of subjects) are missing from Table J. If your N is one of these you should take the next smallest N, e.g. if you had eleven subjects you should look up the row for $N = 10$.)

We have not yet said whether the correlation is significant in the predicted direction. As we obtained a *positive* value of r_s you might assume that this means that there is a *positive* correlation between keenness on outdoor games and an increased number of colds; in fact, the exact *opposite* of the prediction we made that participation in games would lead to *less* colds. But what we have shown is that there is a positive correlation between our rating scores for games and colds. In you look at Table 43, you will see that *high* ratings for colds represent a child with very few colds. So a positive correlation between the rating scores really means that *high* participation in games is correlated with *few* colds. It might have been more convenient to have rated number of colds from 1 (very few) to 5 (very frequent). If you had done so you would have found a negative correlation between games and frequency of colds. You would look up significance levels in Table J in exactly the same way as for a positive r_s, since the probabilities in Table J are concerned with the *size* of a correlation, regardless of whether it has a positive or negative sign.

Question 32
(a) Work out the value of r_s for the rating scores in Table 43, assuming that the games rating scores remain the same while the following rating scores for frequency of colds run from 1 (very few) to 5 (very frequent): 4, 4, 2, 1, 2, 1, 2, 3, 5, 5, 2, 1.
(b) Is there a significant correlation between high participation in outdoor games and low frequency of colds?
(c) What conclusions could you draw about why such a correlation might occur?

9.4   PEARSON PRODUCT MOMENT CORRELATION

When to use

The Pearson product moment correlation is a *parametric* test which measures the amount and significance of a *correlation* between people's scores on *two* variables. Whereas the Spearman test for coefficient can be used with any data, the Pearson requires the experimental data to be measured on an *interval* scale and to meet the other assumptions for parametric tests of being normally distributed and showing homogeneity of variance (see Chapter 7, Sections 7.4 and 7.5).

Example

Suppose you have measured the arithmetic abilities and reading abilities of a group of twelve children by giving them arithmetic and reading tests and got the results shown in Table 44. The prediction is that there is a positive correlation between arithmetic ability and reading ability, i.e. that children who are good readers are also good at arithmetic, children who are average readers are average at arithmetic and children who are poor readers score low on the arithmetic test (a one-tailed hypothesis).

Table 44   Scores on an arithmetic test and a reading test for twelve children

Subject	Variable A (arithmetic score)	Variable B (reading score)	$a \times b$	a^2	b^2
1	32	17	544	1 024	289
2	54	13	702	2 916	169
3	68	14	952	4 624	196
4	93	10	930	8 649	100
5	87	16	1392	7 569	256
6	24	7	168	576	49
7	49	6	294	2 401	36
8	35	18	630	1 225	324
9	97	19	1843	9 409	361
10	62	13	806	3 844	169
11	44	9	396	1 936	81
12	73	12	876	5 329	144
Total	$\sum a = 718$	$\sum b = 154$	$\sum a \times b = 9533$	$\sum a^2 = 49\,502$	$\sum b^2 = 2174$

Rationale

The Pearson test is designed to test whether high scores on one variable tend to be found with high scores on the other variable, low scores with low scores and so on. One advantage with the rank ordering method used for the Spearman test is that it ignores the actual values of the scores on the two variables. Looking back to Table 43 in Section 9.3, it did not matter that there were ten points on the 'games' scale and only five points on the 'colds' scale. In each case high to low ranks could be allocated and compared directly. The Pearson test, on the other hand, does take into account the actual values of the scores when calculating the amount of correlation between two variables. In this case, it obviously does make a difference if the scores for the two variables are measured on different scales. In order to offset this, the degree of association between subjects' scores on the two variables has to be assessed in relation to the overall variability in scores. This total variance is calculated in the usual way by summing squared scores and subtracting a constant.

The statistic r reflects the amount of correlation as a number between -1 (perfect negative correlation) through 0 (no correlation) to $+1$ (perfect positive correlation). The nearer r is to $1(+$ or $-)$ the more likely it is to be significant. So the value of r should be *equal* to or *larger* than the critical values in Table K.

Step-by-Step Instructions for Calculating the Value of _r_

1   For each subject multiply the _A_   See _a_ × _b_ column in Table 44
    variable score by the _B_ variable
    score

2   Square individual scores for vari-   See a^2 and b^2 columns in Table 44
    able _A_ and for variable _B_

3   Find the value of _r_ from the
    formula

$$r = \frac{N \sum a \times b - \sum a \times \sum b}{\sqrt{[N \sum a^2 - (\sum a)^2][\,N \sum b^2 - (\sum b)^2\,]}}$$

where
     N = number of subjects $N = 12$

$\sum a \times b$ = total of $a \times b$ column $\sum a \times b = 9533$

$\sum a$ and $\sum b$ = totals for each $\sum a = 718$
                        variable $\sum b = 154$

$(\sum a)^2$ and $(\sum b)^2$ = totals for $(\sum a)^2 = 718^2$
                       each condition squared $(\sum b)^2 = 154^2$

$\sum a^2$ and $\sum b^2$ = sums of squared $\sum a^2 = 49\,502$
                      individual scores $\sum b^2 = 2174$

$$r = \frac{(12 \times 9533) - (718 \times 154)}{\sqrt{(12 \times 49\,502 - 718^2)(12 \times 2174 - 154^2)}}$$

$$= \frac{114\,396 - 110\,572}{\sqrt{(594\,024 - 515\,524)(26\,088 - 23\,716)}}$$

$$= \frac{3824}{\sqrt{78\,500 \times 2372}}$$

$$= \frac{3824}{\sqrt{186\,202\,000}}$$

$$= \frac{3824}{13\,645.5}$$

$$= .28$$

4   Calculate _df_, i.e. number of sub- $df = N - 2 = 12 - 2 = 10$
    jects minus 2

Looking up Significance in Table K

The top rows of the table show various significance levels for one-tailed and two-tailed tests. In the left-hand column you will find the df (degrees of freedom). For $df = 10$ the observed r value of .28 is smaller than any of the critical values and therefore we cannot conclude that there is a significant correlation between the two variables of arithmetic and reading ability. You will notice that all the values in Table K are positive. If your calculation of r had worked out at $-.28$, you should still look up the significance levels for this negative correlation in Table K, ignoring the sign of the correlation. You should also note that some df are missing. If you had twenty-four subjects ($df = 22$), for instance, you would look up the next smallest df, i.e. $df = 20$.

Question 33

The following scores were obtained from a test for memory for shapes and a test for spelling ability, given to the same ten subjects. Memory for shape scores: 6, 7, 8, 9, 4, 3, 9, 8, 10, 11. Spelling ability scores: 3, 4, 2, 4, 1, 1, 5, 5, 6, 5. It was predicted that there might be a correlation but it might go in either direction.

(a) What is the observed value of r?
(b) Can the experimental hypothesis be accepted at the $p < .001$ level of significance?

Epilogue

Eight chapters—and twelve statistical tests—further on, what might our researcher and sceptical teacher think now? In Chapter 1 they were talking about the *efficiency* of psychological research as a means of studying people's behaviour.

Sceptical teacher   I think you have now convinced me that it is possible to measure the reading performance of children who are given a reading scheme and to use a statistical test to decide whether that performance is *significantly* different from those of other children. I also see how important it is to try and eliminate other irrelevant variables which might be affecting their behaviour.

Researcher   It is kind of you to say so. But I would feel somewhat uneasy if I did not draw your attention to some problems concerning the *interpretation* of the results from an experiment.

Sceptic   You mean what is the 'real' significance of statistically significant results?

Researcher   You remember that accepting a result as being significant at a particular significance level means that there is only a very small probability, say 1% or 5%, that the results might have occurred by a chance combination of other irrelevant variables. But, of course, you can never be certain that this chance event did *not* occur. In fact, even a significance level of $p < .001$ means that there is a 1 in 1000 probability that it might have been a chance result as stated by the null hypothesis.

Sceptic   Is there any way I can guard against this?

Researcher   I am afraid not. Because you can never be 100% certain whether it is the experimental or the null hypothesis which is true, there is always a risk that you might be drawing the wrong conclusions from an experiment. One error you might make is to reject the null hypothesis when it *is* in fact true. This is known as a Type I error. You can think of this as an *optimistic* error, because you are accepting that your results are significant when they are in fact due to chance, since it is the null hypothesis which is true. Another error you might make is to accept the null hypothesis when it is *not* in fact true. This is known as a Type II error. You can think of this as a *pessimistic* error because in this case you are accepting that the results are due to random chance when they are really due to the effects predicted by the experimental hypothesis.

Sceptic   I'm not sure I follow your reasoning here. Are you saying that whatever significance level I accept, I run the risk of making an error?

Researcher   Just think, if one experimenter sets a significance level of

$p < .01$ and another is prepared to accept a significance level of $p < .05$, which of the two is more likely to make a Type II error?

Sceptic   The experimenter who chooses a $p < .01$ significance level is more likely to make a pessimistic Type II error, and the experimenter who chooses a $p < .05$ significance level is more likely to make an optimistic Type I error. To see why, suppose both experimenters found that their results were significant at $p < .02$. The first experimenter would have to accept that his results are not significant because $p < .02$ is a higher probability than $p < .01$. The second experimenter would accept the results as being significant because $p < .02$ is a lower probability than $p < .05$. So from the very *same* results the first experimenter would pessimistically accept the null hypothesis, whereas the second experimenter would optimistically claim significant results although there is a 2% chance that they were not significant at all.

Researcher   Well, I can't help wishing you were in my class of psychology students! The only point to remember is that neither experimenter is 'right' or 'wrong'. The first more cautious experimenter might, for instance, decide that the results of a drug test are not significant and so deprive patients of a drug that has a sporting chance of being beneficial.

Sceptic   But, allowing for this probability angle, can I at least accept that the results of an experiment are due to the variables manipulated by the experimenter?

Researcher   Naturally, I'd like to say yes to this one. But it is not really possible to claim that *all possible* irrelevant variables have been accounted for. I shall give you just one example to show how very difficult it is to be sure that any result is due to the independent variable the experimenter is interested in. Some recent research showed that less of a particular hormone was found in the urine of schizophrenics than in a group of control subjects. This led to a lot of speculation about lack of particular hormones as the cause of schizophrenia. No one had thought of investigating the hospital diet of the schizophrenics. When control subjects were fed the same diet they too produced hormone deficient urine.

Sceptic   And I've just thought of another worry. I seem to remember having read that most experiments investigating psychological processes have been carried out using American university students. If this is true, how can you claim that any results are true of the human population in general?

Researcher   You have a point there. It has been said that all that you learn from many experiments is how students react when asked to do things by their teachers. However, psychologists have become more aware of this problem. Especially in the field of personality and educational research much more effort has gone into making sure that tests of I.Q. or whatever have been validated by testing a sample which is truly representative of the population at large. Another area in which sampling is obviously very important is surveys into people's attitudes or opinions. It is not much use quoting the results of an opinion poll or the market demand for a product if the sample of people questioned does not represent the general opinion.

Sceptic   But what about individual differences? Surely people are so different that you can't draw any conclusions about general laws of behaviour that apply to all human beings?

Researcher   This is one of the really tricky questions for psychologists. In one sense every person is unique. On the other hand, if one insisted that every human being had to be tested individually, it would be impossible to make any general statements about, for instance, the way in which people learn or remember things or the likely effects of introducing a new method for teaching reading.

Sceptic   I see that. But I still can't help feeling that a lot of the experiments described in earlier chapters seem to be far removed from real life behaviour. Can we really learn anything about everyday memory by asking students to remember lists of words?

Researcher   Again, this is a perennial problem for psychological research. It is almost an automatic reflex on the part of an experimenter to standardize the conditions of an experiment so that subjects will be likely to behave in a uniform fashion. The more opportunities subjects have for misinterpreting instructions, interacting in idiosyncratic ways with the experimenter, or reacting to irrelevant variables in the situation, the more general variability there will be in their performance. Nevertheless, it is a good thing for experimenters to remember that, perhaps unfortunately for them—but luckily for the rest of us—variety is the spice of life. Even in the most standardized conditions human beings still tend to react in all sorts of ways.

Sceptic   My reactions to all this are rather muddled. What *are* the advantages and disadvantages of doing *experiments* with human beings?

Researcher   That's the kind of thing I can show best—by producing yet another 'Progress Box'.

Sceptic   What should a psychologist do? Is there a solution?

Researcher   There is no one correct solution. All these 'strengths' and 'weaknesses' represent a trade-off between the precision that comes from experimental controls and a loss of 'real-life' richness. It all depends on the purpose of an experiment, the conditions under which it is going to be carried out, the conclusions which will be drawn from it, and the stage of the research programme. Sometimes it is necessary to rely on intuitive accounts of people's feelings. These may in turn suggest theories about human nature which can be put to a more precise experimental test. But, whatever the aims of a research project, it is obvious that awareness of possible alternative explanations and the various methods of controlling for them are essential skills for any psychologist.

Sceptic Shall we agree, then, that the lot of a psychological researcher is a hard one, but that the attempt to develop methods for the *systematic* study of human beings is a rewarding challenge.

PROGRESS BOX FIFTEEN

Advantages of experiments	*Disadvantages of experiments*
1 Formulation of an experimental hypothesis which predicts a precise relationship between variables	It is not always possible to do this particularly at the exploratory stage of a research programme
2 Manipulating an independent variable to show its effect on a dependent variable	This is not suitable for situations when it is not practically or ethically possible to manipulate a variable
3 Collection of objective, quantitative data which can be statistically analysed to see whether it supports the experimental hypothesis	The psychologist may ignore observational and intuitive evidence which may throw light on human behaviour
4 Elimination of alternative explanations by eliminating irrelevant variables	Control and standardization may result in such an artificial experimental situation that the results have no bearing on real-life behaviour

Answers to Questions

Question 1

(a) The independent variable is whether people are given the illustrated text or the text without illustrations.

(b) The dependent variable is how long it takes people to read the texts.

(c) The experimental hypothesis predicts that people will take less time to read the illustrated text than the non-illustrated text.

(d) The null hypothesis is that the time people take to read a text is due, *not* to whether it is illustrated or not, but to chance fluctuations in people's performance caused by other unknown variables.

Question 2

(a) (1) Smoking results in lung cancer.

(2) A predisposition to lung cancer sets up a craving to smoke.

(3) Another variable, like the anxieties associated with living in big cities, is the cause of both heavy smoking and cancer, although there is no direct link between the two.

(b) Obviously it would be unethical to instruct people to smoke lots of cigarettes to see whether this increased their chance of developing cancer. In fact, many people think it is unethical to do this even with animals. The most that would be possible with humans is to select groups of smokers and non-smokers to study the incidence of cancer. The problem with these kind of self-selected groups is that there may be so many other variables which differentiate between people who choose to smoke and those who do not.

Question 3

(a) The three experimental conditions would be:

Experimental condition 1
   Learning very common words
Experimental condition 2
   Learning less common words
Experimental condition 3
   Learning very rare words

(b) The experimental hypothesis might be that subjects would recall more very common words than less common words and very rare words.

Question 4

	Study time variable	
Type of text variable	*Short study* (2 *min*)	*Long study* (10 *min*)
Passage A (simple sentences)	Condition 1	Condition 2
Passage B (complex sentences)	Condition 3	Condition 4

Question 5

The data support the experimental hypothesis that with a short study time more ideas will be remembered if the sentences are short and simple. If more study time is available, more ideas will be remembered from a more coherent text with longer more complex sentences.

Question 6

(a) The appropriate 2 × 2 table would be:

	Reading scheme 1	*Reading scheme* 2
Backward readers		
Advanced readers		

(b) The four experimental conditions would be:
(1) Reading scheme 1 given to backward readers.
(2) Reading scheme 1 given to advanced readers.
(3) Reading scheme 2 given to backward readers.
(4) Reading scheme 2 given to advanced readers.
N.B. You may have listed the four conditions in a different order and drawn up the 2 × 2 table the other way round (which, of course, is equally correct).

(c) Given the four conditions as listed above, they would fit into the 2 × 2 table as follows:

	Reading scheme 1	*Reading scheme* 2
Backward readers	1	3
Advanced readers	2	4

Question 7

You would need 3 × 3 = 9 experimental conditions.

(1) Simple sentences with short study time.
(2) Simple sentences with medium study time.
(3) Simple sentences with long study time.
(4) Intermediate sentences with short study time.
(5) Intermediate sentences with medium study time.
(6) Intermediate sentences with long study time.
(7) Complex sentences with short study time.
(8) Complex sentences with medium study time.
(9) Complex sentences with long study time.

Question 8

The answer is identical twins. This is because they are alike in heredity (and are always the same sex); so they are likely to be more closely matched than any other pairs of people. Even in this case, however, the match is not perfect since the twins may have been exposed to different environmental conditions, particularly in the rare cases when identical twins are separated from birth.

Question 9

(a) This could only be measured on a nominal scale, grades being allocated into two categories of either pass or fail.

(b) These ratings would be ordinal because they would imply a certain order from best to worse, but it would not be certain that there are equal intervals between the teachers' grades. However, it is common practice for such rating grades to be allotted numbers, implying equal ratings, so that the numbers can be added up and compared on a numerical basis.

(c) Scores on a test are usually treated as *interval* data. However, treating them as interval data makes the assumption that the scores do represent *equal* intervals along a continuous numerical scale of arithmetical ability, i.e. that there is as much difference in the ten percentage points between 20 and 30% as there is between 50 and 60%. It cannot be counted as a *ratio* scale because a score of 0% does not imply nil arithmetic ability—or does it?

Question 10

(a) Four subjects scored 5 correct.
(b) Four subjects scored 4 correct and only two subjects scored 7 correct.
(c) No, because there is no square for 0 correct.
(d) One subject recalled all ten ideas correctly.
(e) Twenty subjects, as represented by the twenty squares in Figure 1, i.e. ten subjects in Condition 1 plus ten subjects in Condition 2.

Question 11

(a) Three subjects.
(b) One subject.
(c) The subjects in Condition 1 recalled more ideas correctly. This is shown by the fact that the squares representing Condition 1 subjects are mostly to be found among the higher numbers of ideas correct (5 or more) while the squares representing Condition 2 subjects are towards the bottom end of ideas correct (5 or less).

(d) Six subjects in Condition 2 had a higher recall score than the subject in Condition 1 who scored only three ideas correct.

Question 12

(a) The correct answer is 1 in 1000.

(b) $p < .001$ (1 in 1000) represents the greatest level of significance since there is only a 1 in 1000 probability that the results of the experiment might have occurred by chance.

Question 13

The easiest way to calculate the mean score for Condition 4 is to work out the totals for each condition.
Condition 1 $4 \times 8 = 32$
Condition 2 $4 \times 12 = 48$
Condition 3 $4 \times 20 = 80$
Condition 4
Total for all subjects $16 \times 16 = 256$
Therefore the total for Condition $4 = 256 - 32 - 48 - 80 = 96$; so the mean score is $96 \div 4 = 24$.

Question 14

The correct ranks are as follows.

Score	Rank
1	2.5
0	1
2	4
1	2.5
3	5

Did you wonder whether you should be ignoring the score of 0? The point is that this represents the score of an individual subject who happened to score 0 in this experiment. This was the lowest score and therefore should be ranked 1. Since the next two scores were both 1, they were allocated the tied ranks of 2.5, the average of the next available ranks of 2 and 3. It is a useful tip to notice that, if you are ranking, say, five scores, the final highest rank should be 5. (Of course, if two subjects had both scored zero they would have been allocated the two lowest tied ranks.)

Question 15

Subject	Condition 1	Condition 2	Difference $(1 - 2)$	Rank
1	3	5	− 2	4
2	5	3	+ 2	4
3	3	2	+ 1	1.5
4	0	5	− 5	7.5
5	4	4	0	—
6	2	5	− 3	6
7	3	5	− 2	4
8	0	0	0	—
9	6	1	+ 5	7.5
10	4	5	− 1	1.5

Notice that the 0 score for subject 4 in Condition 1 is treated as a low score and compared with that same subject's score for Condition 2 to give a difference of − 5. However, the *two* 0 scores for subject 8 result in a *nil* difference in favour of neither condition, as do the two scores of 4 for subject 5. Obviously, if there are too many of these kinds of ties which have to be dropped from the analysis, this severely decreases the chances of getting a significant difference in favour of one condition or the other.

As a consequence of the two ties, a total of eight ranks are available for allocation. But in this case the two last ranks of 7 and 8 are themselves tied to give ranks of 7.5 to the two largest differences of − 5 and + 5 (ignoring the plus and minus signs).

Question 16

(a) The mean scores are 12.5 for Condition 1 and 9.13 for Condition 2.

(b) No. The observed value of $W = 6$ is more than any of the critical values for $N = 7$ (excluding one tie) in Table A. Although there were some quite large plus differences in favour of Condition 1, e.g. + 10 for subject 5 and + 12 for subject 6, the differences between plus and minus ranks were not large enough to achieve a significant result.

Question 17

(a) The experimental hypothesis is one-tailed because it predicts that subjects will find it easier to recognize words presented on the left-hand side of a screen.

(b) See means in table.

Group 1 (eight subjects) (left-hand side)		Group 2 (nine subjects) (right-hand side)	
Score	Rank	Score	Rank
18	17	17	15
15	10.5	13	8
17	15	12	5.5
13	8	16	12.5
11	3.5	10	1.5
16	12.5	15	10.5
10	1.5	11	3.5
17	15	13	8
		12	5.5

Total   117 $T_1 = 83$ Total   119 $T_2 = 70$

Mean   14.63   Mean   13.22

(c) For $U = 8 \times 9 + \dfrac{8 \times (8 + 1)}{2} - 83$

$= 72 + 36 - 83$

$= 25$

For T_2 $U = 8 \times 9 + \dfrac{9 \times (9 + 1)}{2} - 70$

$= 72 + 45 - 70$

$= 47$

The *smaller* $U = 25$. This is not significant because the observed value of $U = 25$ is *larger* than the critical value of 18 for $n_1 = 8$, $n_2 = 9$ in Table B(4) which gives the $p < .05$ probabilities for a one-tailed test.

Question 18

(a) 3.6; 6.6; 7.

(b) Yes. In Table C(1) for $C = 3$, $N = 5$ the critical value for $p < .039$ (a lower probability than $p < .05$) is 6.4. Since the observed value of $\chi_r^2 = 6.7$ is greater than 6.4 we can accept the result as significant at the $p < .05$ level.

Question 19

(a) The mean scores of 9.0 for Condition 1, 4.6 for Condition 2 and 3.4 for Condition 3 are in the direction predicted by the experimental hypothesis but remember that for Page's L you need to put the conditions in the order from predicted *lowest* scores on the left to highest on the right.

(b) No. For $C = 3$, $N = 5$ the observed value of $L = 68$ is smaller than the critical value of 70 for $p < .001$.

(c) Yes. The observed value of $L = 68$ is equal to the critical value of 68 for $p < .01$.

Question 20

(a) 22.25; 32.25; 21.50.

(b) Yes. In Table F for $n_1 = 4$, $n_2 = 4$, $n_3 = 4$ the observed value of $H = 6.125$ is larger than the critical value of 5.6923 for $p < .049$, which is a lower probability than the $p < .05$ significance level.

Question 21

(a) No. For $p < .01$ the observed value of $S = 28$ is *smaller* than the critical value of 32 for $C = 3$, $n = 4$ in Table G. For this test you need to rank predicted scores from lowest on left to highest on right (which in this case reflects better performance in terms of less wrong moves).

(b) Yes. For $p < .05$ the observed value is *larger* than the critical value of 24.

Question 22

Yes. The observed value of $\chi^2 = 12.85$ is larger than the critical value of 9.21 in Table D for 2 *df* at $p < .01$.

Question 23

(a) Yes. At the $p < .005$ (one-tailed) level of significance the critical value of t_{14} in Table H is 2.977. The observed value of 3.613 is *larger* than this critical value and therefore significant.

(b) The observed value of t_7 is 3.156. For a two-tailed hypothesis the critical value of t_7 at $p < .02$ is 2.998 and therefore the observed value of 3.156 is significant at this level (two-tailed).

Question 24

Source of variance	F ratios
Variable A (good or bad spellers)	$\dfrac{\text{variance due to variable } A}{\text{error variance}}$
Variable B (reading Scheme 1 or reading Scheme 2)	$\dfrac{\text{variance due to variable } B}{\text{error variance}}$
Interaction $A \times B$	$\dfrac{\text{variance due to interaction } A \times B}{\text{error variance}}$
Error variance	
Total variance	

Question 25

(a)

Variable B (rate of presentation)	Variable A (type of item)	
	Meaningful words	Nonsense syllables
Fast	5 subjects	5 subjects
Medium	5 subjects	5 subjects
Slow	5 subjects	5 subjects

(b)

Source of variance	Sums of Squares (SS)	Degrees of freedom (df)	Mean Squares (MS)	F Ratios
Variable A (meaningful words or nonsense syllables)	SS	$2 - 1 = 1$	$\dfrac{SS}{1}$	$F_{1,24}\dfrac{MS(A)}{MS(\text{error})}$
Variable B (fast, medium or slow rate)	SS	$3 - 1 = 2$	$\dfrac{SS}{2}$	$F_{2,24}\dfrac{MS(B)}{MS(\text{error})}$
Interaction $A \times B$	SS	$1 \times 2 = 2$	$\dfrac{SS}{2}$	$F_{2,24}\dfrac{MS(A \times B)}{MS(\text{error})}$
Error variance	SS	$29 - 1 - 2 - 2 = 24$	$\dfrac{SS}{24}$	
Total variance	SS	$30 - 1 = 29$		

Question 26

(a)

$$SS_{bet} = \frac{\Sigma T_c^2}{n} - \frac{(\Sigma x)^2}{N} = \frac{30^2 + 17^2}{5} - \frac{47^2}{10} \qquad df = 1$$

$$= 237.8 - 220.9 = 16.9$$

$$SS_{tot} = \Sigma x^2 - \frac{(\Sigma x)^2}{N} = 269 - 220.9 = 48.1 \qquad df = 9$$

$$SS_{error} = SS_{tot} - SS_{bet} = 48.1 - 16.9 = 31.2 \qquad df = 8$$

$$MS_{bet} = \frac{SS_{bet}}{df_{bet}} = \frac{16.9}{1} = 16.9$$

$$MS_{error} = \frac{SS_{error}}{df_{error}} = \frac{31.2}{8} = 3.9$$

$$F_{1,8} = \frac{MS_{bet}}{MS_{error}} = \frac{16.9}{3.9} = 4.33$$

Source of variance	SS	df	MS	F ratio
Between conditions	16.9	1	16.9	$F_{1,8} = 4.33$
Error	31.2	8	3.9	
Total	48.1	9		

(b) The results are not significant in any of the tables.
Note that you could have analysed these data using an unrelated t test since there are only *two* conditions. In fact, the t test and a one-way ANOVA for two conditions will give you identical levels of significance.

(c)
$$SS_{bet} = \frac{50^2 + 50^2 + 50^2 + 50^2}{5} - \frac{200^2}{20}$$

$$= \frac{10000}{5} - \frac{40000}{20}$$

$$= 2000 - 2000 = 0$$

$$SS_{tot} = 10^2 + 10^2 \dots 10^2 - 2000$$

$$= 2000 - 2000 = 0$$

$$SS_{error} = 0 - 0 = 0$$

Not surprisingly, since all scores and totals are the same, there is *no* variability in scores due to differences between conditions nor to differences between individual scores. Consequently all the variances come out as zero.

Question 27

(a)
$$SS_{bet} = \frac{27^2 + 16^2}{5} - \frac{43^2}{10} = 197 - 184.9 = 12.1 \qquad df = 1$$

$$SS_{subj} = \frac{5^2 + 10^2 + 7^2 + 12^2 + 9^2}{2} - 184.9$$

$$= 199.5 - 184.9 = 14.6 \qquad\qquad df = 4$$

$$SS_{tot} = \qquad 221 - 184.9 = 36.1 \qquad\qquad df = 9$$

$$SS_{error} = 36.1 - 12.1 - 14.6 = 9.4 \qquad\qquad df = 4$$

$$MS_{bet} = 12.1$$

$$MS_{subj} = 3.65$$

$$MS_{error} = 2.35$$

(b) $F_{1,4} = 5.148$ conditions not significant; $F_{4,4} = 1.553$ subjects not significant.

Question 28

(a)

Source of variance	SS	df	MS	F ratios
A	14.22	1	14.22	$F_{1,12} = 15.06$
B	4.33	2	2.165	$F_{2,12} = 2.29$
A × B (interaction)	64.12	2	32.06	$F_{2,12} = 33.96$
Error	11.33	12	.944	
Total	94	17		

(b) Yes. Variable A and the interaction of variables $A \times B$ have a significant effect on the scores. The F ratio for variable A, for $v_1 = 1$ and $v_2 = 12$, is significant at the $p < .01$ level (critical value of $F_{1,12} = 9.33$) and the interaction between the two variables is significant at the $p < .001$ level (critical value of $F_{2,12} = 12.97$).

Question 29

The mean for the arithmetic test is 11.25. The mean for the reading test is $3.83 \times 2 = 7.67$. According to these scores this group of children were better at arithmetic. Of course, this begs all sorts of questions about whether the measures for scoring arithmetic ability and reading ability are really comparable.

Question 30

You should have got a graph looking like this.

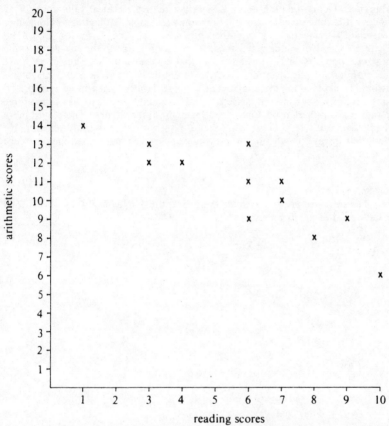

reading scores

The downward slope of the dots shows that there is a tendency for high scores on the arithmetic test to go with low reading scores (at the top left of the slope) and low arithmetic scores to go with high reading scores (at the bottom right of the slope). Notice that there is quite a scatter of dots in the centre of the graph which do not follow the downward slope. This part of the scattergram indicates that there is no particular correlation between reading and arithmetic in this middle range of scores. Children who scored 6 and 7 for reading scored anything from 9 to 13 in arithmetic.

Question 31

The negative correlation of $-.65$ represents the greatest amount of correlation. This is because it is the nearest to $+1$ or -1, both of which mean a perfect correlation (positive and negative, respectively). The 0 represents no correlation at all, i.e. when the scores on the two tests are scattered with no tendency for high and low scores on one variable to go with high or low scores on the other variable. The positive correlation of $+.5$ is quite high, but not as high as $-.65$.

Question 32

(a) $r_s = -.72$.

(b) This (negative) correlation of $-.71$ is larger than the critical value for $N = 12$ of $.591$ for $p < .025$ (one-tailed), which supports the prediction that high scores for games would correlate with *low* scores for numbers of colds.

(c) There is no way of telling whether this correlation is due to the fact that playing outdoor games prevents colds or whether it is that children who have lots of colds are prevented from taking part in games. In order to decide between these two interpretations it would be necessary to manipulate one of the variables. For example, for a period of 3 months one group of randomly selected children could be made to play games three times a week and another group only once a fortnight. If the children who played more games had significantly less colds during that 3-month period, it would be reasonable to suppose that it was the difference in playing games which had caused the difference in number of colds.

Question 33

(a) $r = .86$

(b) Yes. The observed r value is larger than the critical value for $df = 8$ of $r = .7646$ at the $p < .01$ level of significance (two-tailed).

References

Edwards, A. L. (1968) *Experimental Design in Psychological Research*, New York, Holt, Rinehart & Winston Inc. (3rd edn.).

Siegel, S. (1956) *Nonparametric Statistics for the Behavioral Sciences*, New York, McGraw-Hill Book Co. (Int. Student edn).

Winer, B. J. (1962) *Statistical Principles in Experimental Design*, New York, McGraw-Hill Book Co.

Statistical Tables A to K

Table A   Critical values of W at various levels of probability (Wilcoxon)

The statistic W denotes the smaller sum of ranks associated with differences that are all of the same sign. For any N (number of subjects or pairs of matched subjects) the observed value of W is significant at a given level of significance if it is *equal* to or *less* than the critical values shown in the table.

	Level of significance for one-tailed test					Level of significance for one-tailed test			
	.05	.025	.01	.005		.05	.025	.01	.005
	Level of significance for two-tailed test					Level of significance for two-tailed test			
N	.10	.05	.02	.01	N	.10	.05	.02	.01
5	1	—	—	—	28	130	117	102	92
6	2	1	—	—	29	141	127	111	100
7	4	2	0	—	30	152	137	120	109
8	6	4	2	0	31	163	148	130	118
9	8	6	3	2	32	175	159	141	128
10	11	8	5	3	33	188	171	151	138
11	14	11	7	5	34	201	183	162	149
12	17	14	10	7	35	214	195	174	160
13	21	17	13	10	36	228	208	186	171
14	26	21	16	13	37	242	222	198	183
15	30	25	20	16	38	256	235	211	195
16	36	30	24	19	39	271	250	224	208
17	41	35	28	23	40	287	264	238	221
18	47	40	33	28	41	303	279	252	234
19	54	46	38	32	42	319	295	267	248
20	60	52	43	37	43	336	311	281	262
21	68	59	49	43	44	353	327	297	277
22	75	66	56	49	45	371	344	313	292
23	83	73	62	55	46	389	361	329	307
24	92	81	69	61	47	408	379	345	323
25	101	90	77	68	48	427	397	362	339
26	110	98	85	76	49	446	415	380	356
27	120	107	93	84	50	466	434	398	373

*Dashes in the table indicate that no decision is possible at the stated level of significance.

Table B Critical values of U at various levels of probability (Mann–Whitney)

For any n_1 and n_2 the observed value of U is significant at a given level of significance if it is *equal* to or *less* than the critical values shown in the Tables B(1)–(4).

Table B(1) Critical values of U for a one-tailed test at .005; two-tailed test at .01*

											n_1									
n_2	1	2	3	4	5	6	7	8	9	10	11	12	13	14	15	16	17	18	19	20
1	—	—	—	—	—	—	—	—	—	—	—	—	—	—	—	—	—	—	—	—
2	—	—	—	—	—	—	—	—	—	—	—	—	—	—	—	—	—	—	0	0
3	—	—	—	—	—	—	—	—	—	0	0	0	1	1	1	2	2	2	2	3	3
4	—	—	—	—	—	—	0	0	1	1	2	2	3	3	4	5	5	6	6	7	8
5	—	—	—	—	0	1	1	2	3	4	5	6	7	7	8	9	10	11	12	13
6	—	—	—	0	1	2	3	4	5	6	7	9	10	11	12	13	15	16	17	18
7	—	—	—	0	1	3	4	6	7	9	10	12	13	15	16	18	19	21	22	24
8	—	—	—	1	2	4	6	7	9	11	13	15	17	18	20	22	24	26	28	30
9	—	—	0	1	3	5	7	9	11	13	16	18	20	22	24	27	29	31	33	36
10	—	—	0	2	4	6	9	11	13	16	18	21	24	26	29	31	34	37	39	42
11	—	—	0	2	5	7	10	13	16	18	21	24	27	30	33	36	39	42	45	48
12	—	—	1	3	6	9	12	15	18	21	24	27	31	34	37	41	44	47	51	54
13	—	—	1	3	7	10	13	17	20	24	27	31	34	38	42	45	49	53	56	60
14	—	—	1	4	7	11	15	18	22	26	30	34	38	42	46	50	54	58	63	67
15	—	—	2	5	8	12	16	20	24	29	33	37	42	46	51	55	60	64	69	73
16	—	—	2	5	9	13	18	22	27	31	36	41	45	50	55	60	65	70	74	79
17	—	—	2	6	10	15	19	24	29	34	39	44	49	54	60	65	70	75	81	86
18	—	—	2	6	11	16	21	26	31	37	42	47	53	58	64	70	75	81	87	92
19	—	0	3	7	12	17	22	28	33	39	45	51	56	63	69	74	81	87	93	99
20	—	0	3	8	13	18	24	30	36	42	48	54	60	67	73	79	86	92	99	105

*Dashes in the body of the table indicate that no decision is possible at the stated level of significance.

Table B(2) Critical values of U for a one-tailed test at .01; two-tailed test at .02*

										n_1										
n_2	1	2	3	4	5	6	7	8	9	10	11	12	13	14	15	16	17	18	19	20
1	—	—	—	—	—	—	—	—	—	—	—	—	—	—	—	—	—	—	—	—
2	—	—	—	—	—	—	—	—	—	—	—	—	0	0	0	0	0	0	1	1
3	—	—	—	—	—	—	—	0	0	1	1	1	2	2	2	3	3	4	4	4	5
4	—	—	—	—	0	1	1	2	3	3	4	5	5	6	7	7	8	9	9	10
5	—	—	—	0	1	2	3	4	5	6	7	8	9	10	11	12	13	14	15	16
6	—	—	—	1	2	3	4	6	7	8	9	11	12	13	15	16	18	19	20	22
7	—	—	0	1	3	4	6	7	9	11	12	14	16	17	19	21	23	24	26	28
8	—	—	0	2	4	6	7	9	11	13	15	17	20	22	24	26	28	30	32	34
9	—	—	1	3	5	7	9	11	14	16	18	21	23	26	28	31	33	36	38	40
10	—	—	1	3	6	8	11	13	16	19	22	24	27	30	33	36	38	41	44	47
11	—	—	1	4	7	9	12	15	18	22	25	28	31	34	37	41	44	47	50	53
12	—	—	2	5	8	11	14	17	21	24	28	31	35	38	42	46	49	53	56	60
13	—	0	2	5	9	12	16	20	23	27	31	35	39	43	47	51	55	59	63	67
14	—	0	2	6	10	13	17	22	26	30	34	38	43	47	51	56	60	65	69	73
15	—	0	3	7	11	15	19	24	28	33	37	42	47	51	56	61	66	70	75	80
16	—	0	3	7	12	16	21	26	31	36	41	46	51	56	61	66	71	76	82	87
17	—	0	4	8	13	18	23	28	33	38	44	49	55	60	66	71	77	82	88	93
18	—	0	4	9	14	19	24	30	36	41	47	53	59	65	70	76	82	88	94	100
19	—	1	4	9	15	20	26	32	38	44	50	56	63	69	75	82	88	94	101	107
20	—	1	5	10	16	22	28	34	40	47	53	60	67	73	80	87	93	100	107	114

*Dashes in the body of the table indicate that no decision is possible at the stated level of significance.

Table B(3) Critical values of U for a one-tailed test at .025; two-tailed test at .05 *

n_2	1	2	3	4	5	6	7	8	9	10	11	12	13	14	15	16	17	18	19	20
1	—	—	—	—	—	—	—	—	—	—	—	—	—	—	—	—	—	—	—	—
2	—	—	—	—	—	—	—	0	0	0	0	1	1	1	1	1	2	2	2	2
3	—	—	—	—	0	1	1	2	2	3	3	4	4	5	5	6	6	7	7	8
4	—	—	—	0	1	2	3	4	4	5	6	7	8	9	10	11	11	12	13	13
5	—	—	0	1	2	3	5	6	7	8	9	11	12	13	14	15	17	18	19	20
6	—	—	1	2	3	5	6	8	10	11	13	14	16	17	19	21	22	24	25	27
7	—	—	1	3	5	6	8	10	12	14	16	18	20	22	24	26	28	30	32	34
8	—	0	2	4	6	8	10	13	15	17	19	22	24	26	29	31	34	36	38	41
9	—	0	2	4	7	10	12	15	17	20	23	26	28	31	34	37	39	42	45	48
10	—	0	3	5	8	11	14	17	20	23	26	29	33	36	39	42	45	48	52	55
11	—	0	3	6	9	13	16	19	23	26	30	33	37	40	44	47	51	55	58	62
12	—	1	4	7	11	14	18	22	26	29	33	37	41	45	49	53	57	61	65	69
13	—	1	4	8	12	16	20	24	28	33	37	41	45	50	54	59	63	67	72	76
14	—	1	5	9	13	17	22	26	31	36	40	45	50	55	59	64	67	74	78	83
15	—	1	5	10	14	19	24	29	34	39	44	49	54	59	64	70	75	80	85	90
16	—	1	6	11	15	21	26	31	37	42	47	53	59	64	70	75	81	86	92	98
17	—	2	6	11	17	22	28	34	39	45	51	57	63	67	75	81	87	93	99	105
18	—	2	7	12	18	24	30	36	42	48	55	61	67	74	80	86	93	99	106	112
19	—	2	7	13	19	25	32	38	45	52	58	65	72	78	85	92	99	106	113	119
20	—	2	8	13	20	27	34	41	48	55	62	69	76	83	90	98	105	112	119	127

*Dashes in the body of the table indicate that no decision is possible at the stated level of significance.

Table B(4)   Critical values of U for a one-tailed test at .05; two-tailed test at .10*

n_2	1	2	3	4	5	6	7	8	9	10	11	12	13	14	15	16	17	18	19	20
1	—	—	—	—	—	—	—	—	—	—	—	—	—	—	—	—	—	—	0	0
2	—	—	—	—	0	0	0	1	1	1	1	2	2	2	3	3	3	4	4	4
3	—	—	0	0	1	2	2	3	3	4	5	5	6	7	7	8	9	9	10	11
4	—	—	0	1	2	3	4	5	6	7	8	9	10	11	12	14	15	16	17	18
5	—	0	1	2	4	5	6	8	9	11	12	13	15	16	18	19	20	22	23	25
6	—	0	2	3	5	7	8	10	12	14	16	17	19	21	23	25	26	28	30	32
7	—	0	2	4	6	8	11	13	15	17	19	21	24	26	28	30	33	35	37	39
8	—	1	3	5	8	10	13	15	18	20	23	26	28	31	33	36	39	41	44	47
9	—	1	3	6	9	12	15	18	21	24	27	30	33	36	39	42	45	48	51	54
10	—	1	4	7	11	14	17	20	24	27	31	34	37	41	44	48	51	55	58	62
11	—	1	5	8	12	16	19	23	27	31	34	38	42	46	50	54	57	61	65	69
12	—	2	5	9	13	17	21	26	30	34	38	42	47	51	55	60	64	68	72	77
13	—	2	6	10	15	19	24	28	33	37	42	47	51	56	61	65	70	75	80	84
14	—	2	7	11	16	21	26	31	36	41	46	51	56	61	66	71	77	82	87	92
15	—	3	7	12	18	23	28	33	39	44	50	55	61	66	72	77	83	88	94	100
16	—	3	8	14	19	25	30	36	42	48	54	60	65	71	77	83	89	95	101	107
17	—	3	9	15	20	26	33	39	45	51	57	64	70	77	83	89	96	102	109	115
18	—	4	9	16	22	28	35	41	48	55	61	68	75	82	88	95	102	109	116	123
19	0	4	10	17	23	30	37	44	51	58	65	72	80	87	94	101	109	116	123	130
20	0	4	11	18	25	32	39	47	54	62	69	77	84	92	100	107	115	123	130	138

*Dashes in the body of the table indicate that no decision is possible at the stated level of significance.

Table C   Critical values of χ_{r^2} at various levels of probability (Friedman)

For any C and N the observed value of χ_{r^2} is significant at a given level of significance if it is *equal* to or *larger* then the critical values shown in Tables C(1) and C(2).

Table C(1) Critical values for three conditions $(C = 3)$

$N = 2$		$N = 3$		$N = 4$		$N = 5$	
χr^2	p	χr^2	p	χr^2	p	χr^2	p
0	1.000	.000	1.000	.0	1.000	.0	1.000
1	.833	.667	.944	.5	.931	.4	.954
3	.500	2.000	.528	1.5	.653	1.2	.691
4	.167	2.667	.361	2.0	.431	1.6	.522
		4.667	.194	3.5	.273	2.8	.367
		6.000	.028	4.5	.125	3.6	.182
				6.0	.069	4.8	.124
				6.5	.042	5.2	.093
				8.0	.0046	6.4	.039
						7.6	.024
						8.4	.0085
						10.0	.00077

$N = 6$		$N = 7$		$N = 8$		$N = 9$	
χr^2	p	χr^2	p	χr^2	p	χr^2	p
.00	1.000	.000	1.000	.00	1.000	.000	1.000
.33	.956	.286	.964	.25	.967	.222	.971
1.00	.740	.857	.768	.75	.794	.667	.814
1.33	.570	1.143	.620	1.00	.654	.889	.865
2.33	.430	2.000	.486	1.75	.531	1.556	.569
3.00	.252	2.571	.305	2.25	.355	2.000	.398
4.00	.184	3.429	.237	3.00	.285	2.667	.328
4.33	.142	3.714	.192	3.25	.236	2.889	.278
5.33	.072	4.571	.112	4.00	.149	3.556	.187
6.33	.052	5.429	.085	4.75	.120	4.222	.154
7.00	.029	6.000	.052	5.25	.079	4.667	.107
8.33	.012	7.143	.027	6.25	.047	5.556	.069
9.00	.0081	7.714	.021	6.75	.038	6.000	.057
9.33	.0055	8.000	.016	7.00	.030	6.222	.048
10.33	.0017	8.857	.0084	7.75	.018	6.889	.031
12.00	.00013	10.286	.0036	9.00	.0099	8.000	.019
		10.571	.0027	9.25	.0080	8.222	.016
		11.143	.0012	9.75	.0048	8.667	.010
		12.286	.00032	10.75	.0024	9.556	.0060
		14.000	.000021	12.00	.0011	10.667	.0035
				12.25	.00086	10.889	.0029
				13.00	.00026	11.556	.0013
				14.25	.000061	12.667	.00066
				16.00	.0000036	13.556	.00035
						14.000	.00020
						14.222	.000097
						14.889	.000054
						16.222	.000011
						18.000	.0000006

Table C(2) Critical values for four conditions ($C = 4$)

$N = 2$		$N = 3$		$N = 4$			
χr^2	p	χr^2	p	χr^2	p	χr^2	p
.0	1.000	.0	1.000	.0	1.000	5.7	.141
.6	.958	.6	.958	.3	.992	6.0	.105
1.2	.834	1.0	.910	.6	.928	6.3	.094
1.8	.792	1.8	.727	.9	.900	6.6	.077
2.4	.625	2.2	.608	1.2	.800	6.9	.068
3.0	.542	2.6	.524	1.5	.754	7.2	.054
3.6	.458	3.4	.446	1.8	.677	7.5	.052
4.2	.375	3.8	.342	2.1	.649	7.8	.036
4.8	.208	4.2	.300	2.4	.524	8.1	.033
5.4	.167	5.0	.207	2.7	.508	8.4	.019
6.0	.042	5.4	.175	3.0	.432	8.7	.014
		5.8	.148	3.3	.389	9.3	.012
		6.6	.075	3.6	.355	9.6	.0069
		7.0	.054	3.9	.324	9.9	.0062
		7.4	.033	4.5	.242	10.2	.0027
		8.2	.017	4.8	.200	10.8	.0016
		9.0	.0017	5.1	.190	11.1	.00094
				5.4	.158	12.0	.000072

Table D   Critical values of χ^2 at various levels of
probability (chi-square)

For any particular *df* the observed value of χ^2 is
significant at a given level of significance if it is
equal to or *larger* than the critical values shown
in the table.

df	.10	.05	.02	.01	.001
1	2.71	3.84	5.41	6.64	10.83
2	4.60	5.99	7.82	9.21	13.82
3	6.25	7.82	9.84	11.34	16.27
4	7.78	9.49	11.67	13.28	18.46
5	9.24	11.07	13.39	15.09	20.52
6	10.64	12.59	15.03	16.81	22.46
7	12.02	14.07	16.62	18.48	24.32
8	13.36	15.51	18.17	20.09	26.12
9	14.68	16.92	19.68	21.67	27.88
10	15.99	18.31	21.16	23.21	29.59
11	17.28	19.68	22.62	24.72	31.26
12	18.55	21.03	24.05	26.22	32.91
13	19.81	22.36	25.47	27.69	34.53
14	21.06	23.68	26.87	29.14	36.12
15	22.31	25.00	28.26	30.58	37.70
16	23.54	26.30	29.63	32.00	39.29
17	24.77	27.59	31.00	33.41	40.75
18	25.99	28.87	32.35	34.80	42.31
19	27.20	30.14	33.69	36.19	43.82
20	28.41	31.41	35.02	37.57	45.32
21	29.62	32.67	36.34	38.93	46.80
22	30.81	33.92	37.66	40.29	48.27
23	32.01	35.17	38.97	41.64	49.73
24	33.20	36.42	40.27	42.98	51.18
25	34.38	37.65	41.57	44.31	52.62
26	35.56	38.88	42.86	45.64	54.05
27	36.74	40.11	44.14	46.97	55.48
28	37.92	41.34	45.42	48.28	56.89
29	39.09	42.56	46.69	49.59	58.30
30	40.26	43.77	47.96	50.89	59.70

Table E Critical values of Page's L (one-tailed) at various levels of probability

For any N (number of subjects or sets of matched subjects) and C the observed value of L is significant at a given level of significance if it is *equal* to or *larger* than the critical values shown in the table.

| | | C | | | |
| | | *(number of conditions)* | | | |
N	3	4	5	6	$p<$
2	—	—	109	178	.001
	—	60	106	173	.01
	28	58	103	166	.05
3	—	89	160	260	.001
	42	87	155	252	.01
	41	84	150	244	.05
4	56	117	210	341	.001
	55	114	204	331	.01
	54	111	197	321	.05
5	70	145	259	420	.001
	68	141	251	409	.01
	66	137	244	397	.05
6	83	172	307	499	.001
	81	167	299	486	.01
	79	163	291	474	.05
7	96	198	355	577	.001
	93	193	346	563	.01
	91	189	338	550	.05
8	109	225	403	655	.001
	106	220	393	640	.01
	104	214	384	625	.05
9	121	252	451	733	.001
	119	246	441	717	.01
	116	240	431	701	.05
10	134	278	499	811	.001
	131	272	487	793	.01
	128	266	477	777	.05
11	147	305	546	888	.001
	144	298	534	869	.01
	141	292	523	852	.05
12	160	331	593	965	.001
	156	324	581	946	.01
	153	317	570	928	.05

Table F   Critical values of H at various levels of probability (Kruskal–Wallis)

For any n_1, n_2, n_3 the observed value of H is significant at a given level of significance if it is *equal* to or *larger* than the critical values shown in the table.

n_1	n_2	n_3	H	p	n_1	n_2	n_3	H	p
2	1	1	2.7000	.500	4	3	1	5.8333	.021
								5.2083	.050
2	2	1	3.6000	.200				5.0000	.057
								4.0556	.093
2	2	2	4.5714	.067				3.8889	.129
			3.7143	.200					
					4	3	2	6.4444	.008
3	1	1	3.2000	.300				6.3000	.011
								5.4444	.046
3	2	1	4.2857	.100				5.4000	.051
			3.8571	.133				4.5111	.098
								4.4444	.102
3	2	2	5.3572	.029					
			4.7143	.048	4	3	3	6.7455	.010
			4.5000	.067				6.7091	.013
			4.4643	.105				5.7909	.046
								5.7273	.050
3	3	1	5.1429	.043				4.7091	.092
			4.5714	.100				4.7000	.101
			4.0000	.129					
					4	4	1	6.6667	.010
3	3	2	6.2500	.011				6.1667	.022
			5.3611	.032				4.9667	.048
			5.1389	.061				4.8667	.054
			4.5556	.100				4.1667	.082
			4.2500	.121				4.0667	.102
3	3	3	7.2000	.004	4	4	2	7.0364	.006
			6.4889	.011				6.8727	.011
			5.6889	.029				5.4545	.046
			5.6000	.050				5.2364	.052
			5.0667	.086				4.5545	.098
			4.6222	.100				4.4455	.103
4	1	1	3.5714	.200	4	4	3	7.1439	.010
								7.1364	.011
4	2	1	4.8214	.057				5.5985	.049
			4.5000	.076				5.5758	.051
			4.0179	.114				4.5455	.099
								4.4773	.102
4	2	2	6.0000	.014					
			5.3333	.033	4	4	4	7.6538	.008
			5.1250	.052				7.5385	.011
			4.4583	.100				5.6923	.049
			4.1667	.105				5.6538	.054
								4.6539	.097
								4.5001	.104

(continued)

Table F (*continued*)

n_1	n_2	n_3	H	p	n_1	n_2	n_3	H	p
5	1	1	3.8571	.143	5	4	3	7.4449	.010
								7.3949	.011
5	2	1	5.2500	.036				5.6564	.049
			5.0000	.048				5.6308	.050
			4.4500	.071				4.5487	.099
			4.2000	.095				4.5231	.103
			4.0500	.119					
					5	4	4	7.7604	.009
5	2	2	6.5333	.008				7.7440	.011
			6.1333	.013				5.6571	.049
			5.1600	.034				5.6176	.050
			5.0400	.056				4.6187	.100
			4.3733	.090				4.5527	.102
			4.2933	.122					
					5	5	1	7.3091	.009
5	3	1	6.4000	.012				6.8364	.011
			4.9600	.048				5.1273	.046
			4.8711	.052				4.9091	.053
			4.0178	.095				4.1091	.086
			3.8400	.123				4.0364	.105
5	3	2	6.9091	.009	5	5	2	7.3385	.010
			6.8218	.010				7.2692	.010
			5.2509	.049				5.3385	.047
			5.1055	.052				5.2462	.051
			4.6509	.091				4.6231	.097
			4.4945	.101				4.5077	.100
5	3	3	7.0788	.009	5	5	3	7.5780	.010
			6.9818	.011				7.5429	.010
			5.6485	.049				5.7055	.046
			5.5152	.051				5.6264	.051
			4.5333	.097				4.5451	.100
			4.4121	.109				4.5363	.102
5	4	1	6.9545	.008	5	5	4	7.8229	.010
			6.8400	.011				7.7914	.010
			4.9855	.044				5.6657	.049
			4.8600	.056				5.6429	.050
			3.9873	.098				4.5229	.099
			3.9600	.102				4.5200	.101
5	4	2	7.2045	.009	5	5	5	8.0000	.009
			7.1182	.010				7.9800	.010
			5.2727	.049				5.7800	.049
			5.2682	.050				5.6600	.051
			4.5409	.098				4.5600	.100
			4.5182	.101				4.5000	.102

Table G Critical values of S (one-tailed) at various levels of probability (Jonckheere Trend)

For any C and n the observed value of S is significant at a given level of significance if it is *equal* to or *larger* than the critical values shown in the table.

Significance level $p < .05$

n

C	2	3	4	5	6	7	8	9	10
3	10	17	24	33	42	53	64	76	88
4	14	26	38	51	66	82	100	118	138
5	20	34	51	71	92	115	140	166	194
6	26	44	67	93	121	151	184	219	256

Significance level $p < .01$

3	—	23	32	45	59	74	90	106	124
4	20	34	50	71	92	115	140	167	195
5	26	48	72	99	129	162	197	234	274
6	34	62	94	130	170	213	260	309	361

Table H Critical values of t at various levels of probability (t test)

For any particular df the observed value of t is significant at a given level of significance if it is *equal* to or *larger* than the critical values shown in the table.

df	Level of significance for one-tailed test					
	.10	.05	.025	.01	.005	.0005
	Level of significance for two-tailed test					
	.20	.10	.05	.02	.01	.001
1	3.078	6.314	12.706	31.821	63.657	636.619
2	1.886	2.920	4.303	6.965	9.925	31.598
3	1.638	2.353	3.182	4.541	5.841	12.941
4	1.533	2.132	2.776	3.747	4.604	8.610
5	1.476	2.015	2.571	3.365	4.032	6.859
6	1.440	1.943	2.447	3.143	3.707	5.959
7	1.415	1.895	2.365	2.998	3.499	5.405
8	1.397	1.860	2.306	2.896	3.355	5.041
9	1.383	1.833	2.262	2.821	3.250	4.781
10	1.372	1.812	2.228	2.764	3.169	4.587
11	1.363	1.796	2.201	2.718	3.106	4.437
12	1.356	1.782	2.179	2.681	3.055	4.318
13	1.350	1.771	2.160	2.650	3.012	4.221
14	1.345	1.761	2.145	2.624	2.977	4.140
15	1.341	1.753	2.131	2.602	2.947	4.073
16	1.337	1.746	2.120	2.583	2.921	4.015
17	1.333	1.740	2.110	2.567	2.898	3.965
18	1.330	1.734	2.101	2.552	2.878	3.922
19	1.328	1.729	2.093	2.539	2.861	3.883
20	1.325	1.725	2.086	2.528	2.845	3.850
21	1.323	1.721	2.080	2.518	2.831	3.819
22	1.321	1.717	2.074	2.508	2.819	3.792
23	1.319	1.714	2.069	2.500	2.807	3.767
24	1.318	1.711	2.064	2.492	2.797	3.745
25	1.316	1.708	2.060	2.485	2.787	3.725
26	1.315	1.706	2.056	2.479	2.779	3.707
27	1.314	1.703	2.052	2.473	2.771	3.690
28	1.313	1.701	2.048	2.467	2.763	3.674
29	1.311	1.699	2.045	2.462	2.756	3.659
30	1.310	1.697	2.042	2.457	2.750	3.646
40	1.303	1.684	2.021	2.423	2.704	3.551
60	1.296	1.671	2.000	2.390	2.660	3.460
120	1.289	1.658	1.980	2.358	2.617	3.373
∞	1.282	1.645	1.960	2.326	2.576	3.291

N.B. When there is no exact df use the next lowest number, except for very large dfs (well over 120), when you can use the infinity row.

Table I Critical values of F at various levels of probability (F ratios)

For any v_1 and v_2 the observed value of F is significant at a given level of significance if it is *equal* to or *larger* than the critical values shown in Tables I(1)–(4).

Table I(1) Critical values of F at $p < .05$

v_2	v_1 1	2	3	4	5	6	7	8	10	12	24	∞
1	161.4	199.5	215.7	224.6	230.2	234.0	236.8	238.9	241.9	243.9	249.0	254.3
2	18.5	19.0	19.2	19.2	19.3	19.3	19.4	19.4	19.4	19.4	19.5	19.5
3	10.13	9.55	9.28	9.12	9.01	8.94	8.89	8.85	8.79	8.74	8.64	8.53
4	7.71	6.94	6.59	6.39	6.26	6.16	6.09	6.04	5.96	5.91	5.77	5.63
5	6.61	5.79	5.41	5.19	5.05	4.95	4.88	4.82	4.74	4.68	4.53	4.36
6	5.99	5.14	4.76	4.53	4.39	4.28	4.21	4.15	4.06	4.00	3.84	3.67
7	5.59	4.74	4.35	4.12	3.97	3.87	3.79	3.73	3.64	3.57	3.41	3.23
8	5.32	4.46	4.07	3.84	3.69	3.58	3.50	3.44	3.35	3.28	3.12	2.93
9	5.12	4.26	3.86	3.63	3.48	3.37	3.29	3.23	3.14	3.07	2.90	2.71
10	4.96	4.10	3.71	3.48	3.33	3.22	3.14	3.07	2.98	2.91	2.74	2.54
11	4.84	3.98	3.59	3.36	3.20	3.09	3.01	2.95	2.85	2.79	2.61	2.40
12	4.75	3.89	3.49	3.26	3.11	3.00	2.91	2.85	2.75	2.69	2.51	2.30
13	4.67	3.81	3.41	3.18	3.03	2.92	2.83	2.77	2.67	2.60	2.42	2.21
14	4.60	3.74	3.34	3.11	2.96	2.85	2.76	2.70	2.60	2.53	2.35	2.13
15	4.54	3.68	3.29	3.06	2.90	2.79	2.71	2.64	2.54	2.48	2.29	2.07
16	4.49	3.63	3.24	3.01	2.85	2.74	2.66	2.59	2.49	2.42	2.24	2.01
17	4.45	3.59	3.20	2.96	2.81	2.70	2.61	2.55	2.45	2.38	2.19	1.96
18	4.41	3.55	3.16	2.93	2.77	2.66	2.58	2.51	2.41	2.34	2.15	1.92
19	4.38	3.52	3.13	2.90	2.74	2.63	2.54	2.48	2.38	2.31	2.11	1.88
20	4.35	3.49	3.10	2.87	2.71	2.60	2.51	2.45	2.35	2.28	2.08	1.84
21	4.32	3.47	3.07	2.84	2.68	2.57	2.49	2.42	2.32	2.25	2.05	1.81
22	4.30	3.44	3.05	2.82	2.66	2.55	2.46	2.40	2.30	2.23	2.03	1.78
23	4.28	3.42	3.03	2.80	2.64	2.53	2.44	2.37	2.27	2.20	2.00	1.76
24	4.26	3.40	3.01	2.78	2.62	2.51	2.42	2.36	2.25	2.18	1.98	1.73
25	4.24	3.39	2.99	2.76	2.60	2.49	2.40	2.34	2.24	2.16	1.96	1.71
26	4.23	3.37	2.98	2.74	2.59	2.47	2.39	2.32	2.22	2.15	1.95	1.69
27	4.21	3.35	2.96	2.73	2.57	2.46	2.37	2.31	2.20	2.13	1.93	1.67
28	4.20	3.34	2.95	2.71	2.56	2.45	2.36	2.29	2.19	2.12	1.91	1.65
29	4.18	3.33	2.93	2.70	2.55	2.43	2.35	2.28	2.18	2.10	1.90	1.64
30	4.17	3.32	2.92	2.69	2.53	2.42	2.33	2.27	2.16	2.09	1.89	1.62
32	4.15	3.29	2.90	2.67	2.51	2.40	2.31	2.24	2.14	2.07	1.86	1.59
34	4.13	3.28	2.88	2.65	2.49	2.38	2.29	2.23	2.12	2.05	1.84	1.57
36	4.11	3.26	2.87	2.63	2.48	2.36	2.28	2.21	2.11	2.03	1.82	1.55
38	4.10	3.24	2.85	2.62	2.46	2.35	2.26	2.19	2.09	2.02	1.81	1.53
40	4.08	3.23	2.84	2.61	2.45	2.34	2.25	2.18	2.08	2.00	1.79	1.51
60	4.00	3.15	2.76	2.53	2.37	2.25	2.17	2.10	1.99	1.92	1.70	1.39
120	3.92	3.07	2.68	2.45	2.29	2.18	2.09	2.02	1.91	1.83	1.61	1.25
∞	3.84	3.00	2.60	2.37	2.21	2.10	2.01	1.94	1.83	1.75	1.52	1.00

N.B. When there is no exact number for the df, use the next lowest number. For very large dfs (well over 120) you can use the row for infinity (∞).

Table I(2) Critical values of F at $p < .025$

v_2	v_1											
	1	2	3	4	5	6	7	8	10	12	24	∞
1	648	800	864	900	922	937	948	957	969	977	997	1018
2	38.5	39.0	39.2	39.2	39.3	39.3	39.4	39.4	39.4	39.4	39.5	39.5
3	17.4	16.0	15.4	15.1	14.9	14.7	14.6	14.5	14.4	14.3	14.1	13.9
4	12.22	10.65	9.98	9.60	9.36	9.20	9.07	8.98	8.84	8.75	8.51	8.26
5	10.01	8.43	7.76	7.39	7.15	6.98	6.85	6.76	6.62	6.52	6.28	6.02
6	8.81	7.26	6.60	6.23	5.99	5.82	5.70	5.60	5.46	5.37	5.12	4.85
7	8.07	6.54	5.89	5.52	5.29	5.12	4.99	4.90	4.76	4.67	4.42	4.14
8	7.57	6.06	5.42	5.05	4.82	4.65	4.53	4.43	4.30	4.20	3.95	3.67
9	7.21	5.71	5.08	4.72	4.48	4.32	4.20	4.10	3.96	3.87	3.61	3.33
10	6.94	5.46	4.83	4.47	4.24	4.07	3.95	3.85	3.72	3.62	3.37	3.08
11	6.72	5.26	4.63	4.28	4.04	3.88	3.76	3.66	3.53	3.43	3.17	2.88
12	6.55	5.10	4.47	4.12	3.89	3.73	3.61	3.51	3.37	3.28	3.02	2.72
13	6.41	4.97	4.35	4.00	3.77	3.60	3.48	3.39	3.25	3.15	2.89	2.60
14	6.30	4.86	4.24	3.89	3.66	3.50	3.38	3.29	3.15	3.05	2.79	2.49
15	6.20	4.76	4.15	3.80	3.58	3.41	3.29	3.20	3.06	2.96	2.70	2.40
16	6.12	4.69	4.08	3.73	3.50	3.34	3.22	3.12	2.99	2.89	2.63	2.32
17	6.04	4.62	4.01	3.66	3.44	3.28	3.16	3.06	2.92	2.82	2.56	2.25
18	5.98	4.56	3.95	3.61	3.38	3.22	3.10	3.01	2.87	2.77	2.50	2.19
19	5.92	4.51	3.90	3.56	3.33	3.17	3.05	2.96	2.82	2.72	2.45	2.13
20	5.87	4.46	3.86	3.51	3.29	3.13	3.01	2.91	2.77	2.68	2.41	2.09
21	5.83	4.42	3.82	3.48	3.25	3.09	2.97	2.87	2.73	2.64	2.37	2.04
22	5.79	4.38	3.78	3.44	3.22	3.05	2.93	2.84	2.70	2.60	2.33	2.00
23	5.75	4.35	3.75	3.41	3.18	3.02	2.90	2.81	2.67	2.57	2.30	1.97
24	5.72	4.32	3.72	3.38	3.15	2.99	2.87	2.78	2.64	2.54	2.27	1.94
25	5.69	4.29	3.69	3.35	3.13	2.97	2.85	2.75	2.61	2.51	2.24	1.91
26	5.66	4.27	3.67	3.33	3.10	2.94	2.82	2.73	2.59	2.49	2.22	1.88
27	5.63	4.24	3.65	3.31	3.08	2.92	2.80	2.71	2.57	2.47	2.19	1.85
28	5.61	4.22	3.63	3.29	3.06	2.90	2.78	2.69	2.55	2.45	2.17	1.83
29	5.59	4.20	3.61	3.27	3.04	2.88	2.76	2.67	2.53	2.43	2.15	1.81
30	5.57	4.18	3.59	3.25	3.03	2.87	2.75	2.65	2.51	2.41	2.14	1.79
32	5.53	4.15	3.56	3.22	3.00	2.84	2.72	2.62	2.48	2.38	2.10	1.75
34	5.50	4.12	3.53	3.19	2.97	2.81	2.69	2.59	2.45	2.35	2.08	1.72
36	5.47	4.09	3.51	3.17	2.94	2.79	2.66	2.57	2.43	2.33	2.05	1.69
38	5.45	4.07	3.48	3.15	2.92	2.76	2.64	2.55	2.41	2.31	2.03	1.66
40	5.42	4.05	3.46	3.13	2.90	2.74	2.62	2.53	2.39	2.29	2.01	1.64
60	5.29	3.93	3.34	3.01	2.79	2.63	2.51	2.41	2.27	2.17	1.88	1.48
120	5.15	3.80	3.23	2.89	2.67	2.52	2.39	2.30	2.16	2.05	1.76	1.31
∞	5.02	3.69	3.12	2.79	2.57	2.41	2.29	2.19	2.05	1.94	1.64	1.00

Table I(3)   Critical values of F at $p < .01$

v_2	1	2	3	4	5	6	7	8	10	12	24	∞
							v_1					
1	4052	5000	5403	5625	5764	5859	5928	5981	6056	6106	6235	6366
2	98.5	99.0	99.2	99.2	99.3	99.3	99.4	99.4	99.4	99.4	99.5	99.5
3	34.1	30.8	29.5	28.7	28.2	27.9	27.7	27.5	27.2	27.1	26.6	26.1
4	21.2	18.0	16.7	16.0	15.5	15.2	15.0	14.8	14.5	14.4	13.9	13.5
5	16.26	13.27	12.06	11.39	10.97	10.67	10.46	10.29	10.05	9.89	9.47	9.02
6	13.74	10.92	9.78	9.15	8.75	8.47	8.26	8.10	7.87	7.72	7.31	6.88
7	12.25	9.55	8.45	7.85	7.46	7.19	6.99	6.84	6.62	6.47	6.07	5.65
8	11.26	8.65	7.59	7.01	6.63	6.37	6.18	6.03	5.81	5.67	5.28	4.86
9	10.56	8.02	6.99	6.42	6.06	5.80	5.61	5.47	5.26	5.11	4.73	4.31
10	10.04	7.56	6.55	5.99	5.64	5.39	5.20	5.06	4.85	4.71	4.33	3.91
11	9.65	7.21	6.22	5.67	5.32	5.07	4.89	4.74	4.54	4.40	4.02	3.60
12	9.33	6.93	5.95	5.41	5.06	4.82	4.64	4.50	4.30	4.16	3.78	3.36
13	9.07	6.70	5.74	5.21	4.86	4.62	4.44	4.30	4.10	3.96	3.59	3.17
14	8.86	6.51	5.56	5.04	4.70	4.46	4.28	4.14	3.94	3.80	3.43	3.00
15	8.68	6.36	5.42	4.89	4.56	4.32	4.14	4.00	3.80	3.67	3.29	2.87
16	8.53	6.23	5.29	4.77	4.44	4.20	4.03	3.89	3.69	3.55	3.18	2.75
17	8.40	6.11	5.18	4.67	4.34	4.10	3.93	3.79	3.59	3.46	3.08	2.65
18	8.29	6.01	5.09	4.58	4.25	4.01	3.84	3.71	3.51	3.37	3.00	2.57
19	8.18	5.93	5.01	4.50	4.17	3.94	3.77	3.63	3.43	3.30	2.92	2.49
20	8.10	5.85	4.94	4.43	4.10	3.87	3.70	3.56	3.37	3.23	2.86	2.42
21	8.02	5.78	4.87	4.37	4.04	3.81	3.64	3.51	3.31	3.17	2.80	2.36
22	7.95	5.72	4.82	4.31	3.99	3.76	3.59	3.45	3.26	3.12	2.75	2.31
23	7.88	5.66	4.76	4.26	3.94	3.71	3.54	3.41	3.21	3.07	2.70	2.26
24	7.82	5.61	4.72	4.22	3.90	3.67	3.50	3.36	3.17	3.03	2.66	2.21
25	7.77	5.57	4.68	4.18	3.86	3.63	3.46	3.32	3.13	2.99	2.62	2.17
26	7.72	5.53	4.64	4.14	3.82	3.59	3.42	3.29	3.09	2.96	2.58	2.13
27	7.68	5.49	4.60	4.11	3.78	3.56	3.39	3.26	3.06	2.93	2.55	2.10
28	7.64	5.45	4.57	4.07	3.75	3.53	3.36	3.23	3.03	2.90	2.52	2.06
29	7.60	5.42	4.54	4.04	3.73	3.50	3.33	3.20	3.00	2.87	2.49	2.03
30	7.56	5.39	4.51	4.02	3.70	3.47	3.30	3.17	2.98	2.84	2.47	2.01
32	7.50	5.34	4.46	3.97	3.65	3.43	3.26	3.13	2.93	2.80	2.42	1.96
34	7.45	5.29	4.42	3.93	3.61	3.39	3.22	3.09	2.90	2.76	2.38	1.91
36	7.40	5.25	4.38	3.89	3.58	3.35	3.18	3.05	2.86	2.72	2.35	1.87
38	7.35	5.21	4.34	3.86	3.54	3.32	3.15	3.02	2.83	2.69	2.32	1.84
40	7.31	5.18	4.31	3.83	3.51	3.29	3.12	2.99	2.80	2.66	2.29	1.80
60	7.08	4.98	4.13	3.65	3.34	3.12	2.95	2.82	2.63	2.50	2.12	1.60
120	6.85	4.79	3.95	3.48	3.17	2.96	2.79	2.66	2.47	2.34	1.95	1.38
∞	6.63	4.61	3.78	3.32	3.02	2.80	2.64	2.51	2.32	2.18	1.79	1.00

Table I(4) Critical values of F at $p < .001$

v_2	v_1											
	1	2	3	4	5	6	7	8	10	12	24	∞
1*	4053	5000	5404	5625	5764	5859	5929	5981	6056	6107	6235	6366*
2	998.5	999.0	999.2	999.2	999.3	999.3	999.4	999.4	999.4	999.4	999.5	999.5
3	167.0	148.5	141.1	137.1	134.6	132.8	131.5	130.6	129.2	128.3	125.9	123.5
4	74.14	61.25	56.18	53.44	51.71	50.53	49.66	49.00	48.05	47.41	45.77	44.05
5	47.18	37.12	33.20	31.09	29.75	28.83	28.16	27.65	26.92	26.42	25.14	23.79
6	35.51	27.00	23.70	21.92	20.80	20.03	19.46	19.03	18.41	17.99	16.90	15.75
7	29.25	21.69	18.77	17.20	16.21	15.52	15.02	14.63	14.08	13.71	12.73	11.70
8	25.42	18.49	15.83	14.39	13.48	12.86	12.40	12.05	11.54	11.19	10.30	9.34
9	22.86	16.39	13.90	12.56	11.71	11.13	10.69	10.37	9.87	9.57	8.72	7.81
10	21.04	14.91	12.55	11.28	10.48	9.93	9.52	9.20	8.74	8.44	7.64	6.76
11	19.69	13.81	11.56	10.35	9.58	9.05	8.66	8.35	7.92	7.63	6.85	6.00
12	18.64	12.97	10.80	9.63	8.89	8.38	8.00	7.71	7.29	7.00	6.25	5.42
13	17.82	12.31	10.21	9.07	8.35	7.86	7.49	7.21	6.80	6.52	5.78	4.97
14	17.14	11.78	9.73	8.62	7.92	7.44	7.08	6.80	6.40	6.13	5.41	4.60
15	16.59	11.34	9.34	8.25	7.57	7.09	6.74	6.47	6.08	5.81	5.10	4.31
16	16.12	10.97	9.01	7.94	7.27	6.80	6.46	6.19	5.81	5.55	4.85	4.06
17	15.72	10.66	8.73	7.68	7.02	6.56	6.22	5.96	5.58	5.32	4.63	3.85
18	15.38	10.39	8.49	7.46	6.81	6.35	6.02	5.76	5.39	5.13	4.45	3.67
19	15.08	10.16	8.28	7.27	6.62	6.18	5.85	5.59	5.22	4.97	4.29	3.51
20	14.82	9.95	8.10	7.10	6.46	6.02	5.69	5.44	5.08	4.82	4.15	3.38
21	14.59	9.77	7.94	6.95	6.32	5.88	5.56	5.31	4.95	4.70	4.03	3.26
22	14.38	9.61	7.80	6.81	6.19	5.76	5.44	5.19	4.83	4.58	3.92	3.15
23	14.19	9.47	7.67	6.70	6.08	5.65	5.33	5.09	4.73	4.48	3.82	3.05
24	14.03	9.34	7.55	6.59	5.98	5.55	5.23	4.99	4.64	4.39	3.74	2.97
25	13.88	9.22	7.45	6.49	5.89	5.46	5.15	4.91	4.56	4.31	3.66	2.89
26	13.74	9.12	7.36	6.41	5.80	5.38	5.07	4.83	4.48	4.24	3.59	2.82
27	13.61	9.02	7.27	6.33	5.73	5.31	5.00	4.76	4.41	4.17	3.52	2.75
28	13.50	8.93	7.19	6.25	5.66	5.24	4.93	4.69	4.35	4.11	3.46	2.69
29	13.39	8.85	7.12	6.19	5.59	5.18	4.87	4.64	4.29	4.05	3.41	2.64
30	13.29	8.77	7.05	6.12	5.53	5.12	4.82	4.58	4.24	4.00	3.36	2.59
32	13.12	8.64	6.94	6.01	5.43	5.02	4.72	4.48	4.14	3.91	3.27	2.50
34	12.97	8.52	6.83	5.92	5.34	4.93	4.63	4.40	4.06	3.83	3.19	2.42
36	12.83	8.42	6.74	5.84	5.26	4.86	4.56	4.33	3.99	3.76	3.12	2.35
38	12.71	8.33	6.66	5.76	5.19	4.79	4.49	4.26	3.93	3.70	3.06	2.29
40	12.61	8.25	6.59	5.70	5.13	4.73	4.44	4.21	3.87	3.64	3.01	2.23
60	11.97	7.77	6.17	5.31	4.76	4.37	4.09	3.86	3.54	3.32	2.69	1.89
120	11.38	7.32	5.78	4.95	4.42	4.04	3.77	3.55	3.24	3.02	2.40	1.54
∞	10.83	6.91	5.42	4.62	4.10	3.74	3.47	3.27	2.96	2.74	2.13	1.00

*Entries for $v_2 = 1$ must be multiplied by 100.

Table J Critical values of r_s (rho) at various levels of probability (Spearman rank correlation coefficient)

For any N the observed value of r_s is significant at a given level of significance if it is *equal* to or *larger* than the critical values shown in the table

N	Level of significance for one-tailed test			
	.05	.025	.01	.005
(number of subjects)	Level of significance for two-tailed test			
	.10	.05	.02	.01
5	.900	1.000	1.000	—
6	.829	.886	.943	1.000
7	.714	.786	.893	.929
8	.643	.738	.833	.881
9	.600	.683	.783	.833
10	.564	.648	.746	.794
12	.506	.591	.712	.777
14	.456	.544	.645	.715
16	.425	.506	.601	.665
18	.399	.475	.564	.625
20	.377	.450	.534	.591
22	.359	.428	.508	.562
24	.343	.409	.485	.537
26	.329	.392	.465	.515
28	.317	.377	.448	.496
30	.306	.364	.432	.478

N.B. When there is no exact number of subjects use the next lowest number.

Table K Critical values of *r* at various levels of probability (Pearson product moment correlation)

For any particular of the observed value of *r* is significant at a given level of significance if it is *equal* to or *larger* than the critical values shown in the table

	Level of significance for one-tailed test				
	.05	.025	.01	.005	.0005
	Level of significance for two-tailed test				
$df = N - 2$	.10	.05	.02	.01	.001
1	.9877	.9969	.9995	.9999	1.0000
2	.9000	.9500	.9800	.9900	.9990
3	.8054	.8783	.9343	.9587	.9912
4	.7293	.8114	.8822	.9172	.9741
5	.6694	.7545	.8329	.8745	.9507
6	.6215	.7067	.7887	.8343	.9249
7	.5822	.6664	.7498	.7977	.8982
8	.5494	.6319	.7155	.7646	.8721
9	.5214	.6021	.6851	.7348	.8471
10	.4973	.5760	.6581	.7079	.8233
11	.4762	.5529	.6339	.6835	.8010
12	.4575	.5324	.6120	.6614	.7800
13	.4409	.5139	.5923	.6411	.7603
14	.4259	.4973	.5742	.6226	.7420
15	.4124	.4821	.5577	.6055	.7246
16	.4000	.4683	.5425	.5897	.7084
17	.3887	.4555	.5285	.5751	.6932
18	.3783	.4438	.5155	.5614	.6787
19	.3687	.4329	.5034	.5487	.6652
20	.3598	.4227	.4921	.5368	.6524
25	.3233	.3809	.4451	.4869	.5974
30	.2960	.3494	.4093	.4487	.5541
35	.2746	.3246	.3810	.4182	.5189
40	.2573	.3044	.3578	.3932	.4896
45	.2428	.2875	.3384	.3721	.4648
50	.2306	.2732	.3218	.3541	.4433
60	.2108	.2500	.2948	.3248	.4078
70	.1954	.2319	.2737	.3017	.3799
80	.1829	.2172	.2565	.2830	.3568
90	.1726	.2050	.2422	.2673	.3375
100	.1638	.1946	.2301	.2540	.3211

N.B. When there is no exact *df* use the next lowest number.